RICHARD MACKE[...] educated in London. He was an English exhibitioner at Cambridge University, and President of the Footlights Club. After a short spell as an actor, he became one of the first men ever to be employed on a national "agony" column, working with Claire Rayner and Angela Willans for *Woman's Own*. During this time, he began training in counselling, and continued his interest in the field of human problems during three years reading theology at Cuddesdon College, Oxford.

After ordination, he worked in parishes in central London, and was nominated by the London *Standard* as one of the ten best preachers in the capital.

He is currently Director of Studies in the Ministry and Mission of the Church at Westcott House, Cambridge. He is also much in demand as a speaker, preacher and broadcaster, and is spending an increasing amount of time working with clergy from all denominations, and continuing his work in counselling.

RICHARD MACKENNA

Is There Anyone There?

Collins
FOUNT PAPERBACKS

First published in Great Britain in 1987
by Fount Paperbacks, London

Copyright © Richard MacKenna 1987

Made and printed in Great Britain by
William Collins Sons & Co Ltd, Glasgow

For Robert,
and for Elias and Alex.
With thanks for "laughter and the love of friends"

Contents

Trailer

"In space", yelled the adverts for the horror movie, "no one can hear you scream". Once inside the cinema, it turned out that no one could hear you screaming there either – they were all too busy gasping or groaning or burying their faces in their neighbour's shoulder. The film gave the classic horror situation: take a group of people, isolate them miles from anywhere, and then introduce the murderer . . . But in this case, the unfortunate victims were on a spaceship, light years from our solar system, and the villain was not Colonel Mustard or Miss Marple's next-door neighbour, but a monster with the unpleasant habit of exploding out of people's stomachs or eating them alive.

Now hopefully, no one reading this has had the unnerving experience of being isolated deep in outer space, with a murderous space monster as their only companion. But is it only in space that no one can hear you scream? We have problems enough of our own, and I have the uneasy feeling that a lot of us spend quite a lot of our lives trying to cope with situations that may not be as dramatic as a battle to the death with a monster, but may well feel just as unpleasant. There is a sense of loneliness and isolation as we try to face up to the thing that confronts us, or else as we try to get on with the grey slog of day-to-day living. We're not lost in space, but in the office, the home or the street. And no one seems to hear us screaming either.

Or is it that we're too polite to scream? You don't have to spend very long listening to people under stress, before you become aware that the almost constant refrain, repeated by person after person, is "I thought I must be the only one to feel like this", or "You must think I'm very peculiar/mad/strange/silly". But all they're talking about is normal human emotion – the feelings that they would be mad NOT to have.

It's as if we're all suffering from an inferiority complex: everyone else is normal; no one else is screaming; I must be the odd one out. And yet, if we could take the roofs off the houses, perhaps we'd find that almost everyone is grappling with their own private monster, and perhaps everyone is thinking "I'm the only one to feel like this".

In the movie, the hero, shortly before his death, goes to the all-knowing computer for help. Up until now, the computer has been very useful. Not for nothing is it known as "Mother", as it steers the spaceship, watches over the sleeping astronauts, and generally seems to make life as easy and uncomplicated as possible for them. It is only when trouble comes that you realize that "Mother" is not as concerned about the welfare of her "children" as she might be. Facing almost certain death, the spaceship captain goes to her for help, and their "conversation" runs roughly as follows:

"Request evaluation of current procedure to terminate alien."

"Unable to compute – available data insufficient."

"Request options for possible procedure."

"Unable to compute – available data insufficient."

"What are my chances?"

"Does not compute."

Later on, we discover that it was "Mother" who had been instrumental in getting the alien on board in the first place. Her first loyalty was to The Company who own the spaceship, and who wanted to get their hands on the monster, thinking that it might make a very useful addition to the range of armaments that they peddle.

Now at first sight, you wouldn't think that we have to

10

grapple with unfriendly computers — unless, of course, you've ever had your cash-card eaten by the cash-dispenser outside the bank, or tried to cancel your subscription to the *Reader's Digest*. The problem is that we carry the computer around inside us. We've all been programmed from the day of our birth to believe and expect certain things. But all too often, the programming is faulty, or else it isn't as "user friendly" as it would like us to believe. "Life", it assures us firmly, "is not the way you think it is. There must be something wrong with you. That isn't a monster who wants to gobble you up, but on the contrary it's a very valuable addition to my collection. Perhaps you ought to go and see a psychiatrist/talk to your priest/take up a hobby/swallow another couple of Valium." What we experience is too complex, too ambiguous to fit into the neat programming — or else, possibly, our computer has a vested interest in denying what we feel. Either way, we are left with the difficult decision of whether to obey our programming, which may well have made life fairly simple and uncomplicated for us in the past, or whether to trust our own instincts and say that what we feel and what we experience is real and has meaning. But who are we to argue with all the logic and power of the computer?

And so we go on, because we're obedient little souls really, and we've been well trained to do what we think is expected of us. It was on a T-shirt in New York that I read the message "Life is hard . . . and then you die". "Oho, nonsense!" I thought, grimly cramming another cigarette into my mouth. And "Oho, nonsense!" go the various computer programmes as they stir into action. There's the one which says, "You have an attractive wife and two children; you have nearly paid off the mortgage on your centrally-heated semi; you have a job, and two hundred shares in British Gas and the TSB — of course you don't feel there's something missing." (This programme is almost infinitely extendable, and can also cover yachts, Rolls Royces, and cottages in the Dordogne.) Almost all the programmes go into action when we start feeling emotion. Anger, despair, grief – the fact that at this moment you could cheerfully never see your husband or children again . . . anything which seems to contradict the neatly ordered computer directives, and we start to think "There's something wrong with me", instead of perhaps wondering whether there's something wrong with the computer.

But it takes an emormous amount of courage to try to ignore these old tapes playing away inside us – to dare to say, "What I am, what I feel, is normal".

It was Stevie Smith who used the image of the swimmer in the water, far out from the shore, arms desperately flailing as they tried to call for help:

> I was much too far out all my life
> And not waving but drowning.

Like people, on the beach, we wave back. What a lovely day for a swim! No one else, apart from us, ever gets into deep water, except of course the casualties we see on television or read about in the newspaper. Unemployed black youngsters or drug addicts or famine victims suffer; but nearly everyone else is OK – except for me, but then my computer tells me I'm wrong to feel this way. And whether we're standing on the beach watching, or choking as we feel the current of life pulling us under, still there's a remarkable absence of cries for help: and a remarkable absence of those who are prepared to hear the cries.

*

But if we start trying really to listen to our own lives – and to listen to others – what can we rely on, if not the voices of our programming? "You live in the perfect State, where all are equal and everything exists for your benefit – if you want to get out, then you must be mentally ill." "You have all the material benefits of the most advanced civilization the world has ever known; you must be mad to smoke crack/snort coke/need a couple of stiff drinks before you can relax/leave your husband/beat your wife/feel that there's got to be something better than this."

Talk of something better sets rolling one of the oldest programmes of all. For most people it has been superseded by new generations of software, be they Possessions, Class Warfare, Drugs, Sex, Power, Politics, Liverpool or Yoga. But it's still there, somewhere in the memory banks, perhaps only activated in times of greatest stress. For simplicity, let's call it "God".

Forgive an ultra-long quote, from someone with an even longer name, but perhaps Kierkegaard is posing the sort of question that sets the God programme running:

Listen to the newborn infant's cry in the hour of birth – see the death struggles in the final hour – and then declare whether what begins and ends in this way can be intended to be enjoyment.

True enough, we human beings do everything as fast as possible to get away from these two points, hurry as fast as possible to forget the birth-cry and change it to delight in having given a being life. And when someone dies we immediately say: Softly and gently he slipped away, death is a sleep, a quiet sleep – something we do not say for the sake of the one who died, for our talking cannot help him, but for our own sake, in order not to lose any of the zest for life, in order to change everything to serve an increase in the zest for life during the interval between the birth-cry and the death-wail, between the mother's shriek and the child's repetition of it, when the child at some time dies.

Imagine somewhere a great and splendid hall where everything is done to produce joy and merriment – but the entrance to this room is a nasty, muddy, horrible stairway and it is impossible to pass without getting disgustingly soiled, and admission is paid by prostituting oneself, and when day dawns the merriment is over and all ends with one's being kicked out again – but the whole night through everything is done to keep up and inflame the merriment and pleasure!

What is reflection? Simply to reflect on these two questions: How did I get into this and this, and how do I get out of it again, how does it end? What is thoughtlessness? To muster everything in order to drown all this about entrance and exit in forgetfulness, to muster everything to re-explain and explain away entrance and exit, simply lost in the interval between the birth-cry and the repetition of this cry when the one who is born expires in the death struggle.

Or perhaps W. B. Yeats puts it more simply:

> I balanced all, brought all to mind,
> The years to come seemed waste of breath,
> A waste of breath the years behind
> In balance with this life, this death.

And then the tape starts running, slowly at first but gradually gathering speed . . . "There is an answer. The answer is called God. You can't expect to understand about Him, but there are very wise people who do, and who always look incredibly happy. You must listen to what they say, and obey what they ask. You must get involved in something called Religion. If you promise to be good, to believe what they tell you, and to stop having naughty thoughts, then God will look after you. And to make up for life being such a

14

complicated let-down, there is a personal guarantee that if you will only ever use this programme for the rest of your life, then you will win The Prize . . . you will live for ever." In its most disgusting form, this comes up as little boys being told that if they will walk unarmed onto the enemy guns, then they will die a martyr's death and go straight to paradise. In Iran girl dissidents are raped as a matter of course, because, by losing their virginity, they will be denied the hope of heaven. (I'm sure the soldiers don't enjoy that, do they? They're just doing their religious duty.)

We'll skate over Northern Ireland, the Lebanon, India, the bombing of synagogues, racially segregated churches, etc., etc., etc., because perhaps they feel a bit far from home. But it is as well to remember before we start, that the religious programme, once playing, can be infinitely more vicious and deadly than any alien space monster.

But does this mean that all religion is dangerous? Yes, and no. Yes, if we just let the old tapes play without ever thinking or questioning what they may be about; or if we willingly surrender ourselves to be programmed by someone else, in order to gain a little peace of mind. No, if we can say that life – existence – is religious, with or without religion.

If that sounds like the beginning of an Irish joke, it isn't meant to be. Religion means more than a draughty building containing a few people in Sunday best, listening to an elderly bachelor pontificating about family life. The Religions, the official, organized, man-made institutions, can sometimes obscure religion itself – the religious quest: the search for meaning. No one is quite sure of the origin of the word "religion", but one possibility is that it meant a gathering and tying together – almost as you might tie up a bunch of sticks. But that's an activity that we're all engaged in. Not gathering sticks, but searching for and sorting out and trying to make sense of all the myriad different parts that go to make up our lives.

You might say that the religious question comes down to "What can I believe in, what can I have faith in, in my life?"; even, "What, if anything, is most real in my life?"; even, "What is real?" But if we are going to ask questions like that, who can we trust to give us an answer? That is, always supposing there is an answer to be found.

And here we come to a parting of the ways. Because I want to say that anyone who asks questions like that is involved in the religious task. Anyone who uses language about "God" isn't necessarily talking about a person or a thing. They are talking about worth and value; about the fact that they take themselves and other beings with total seriousness. In human life, in suffering, in the values of the human heart, they find questions of ultimate meaning – and, maybe, hints of answers. The parting of the ways comes for those who would have to say that life is tragic (or sick) because there is no meaning there. Also, perhaps, for those who won't bear with me if I use the idea of religion in such a loose way, or the idea of God.

But human life is religious, with or without religion. And by life, I mean ALL of our life; everything, lock, stock and barrel, every nook and cranny, and any other cliché you can think of to mean the whole thing. God, religion, us – all are involved in the most basic search of all, to find out what it means to be human; to find our meaning.

So who do we trust for answers? In the horror film the last surviving crew-member of the spaceship Nostromo is left alone to confront the monster which has destroyed her companions. The computer, all the wonders of science, are at best neutral spectators of the conflict. All that she has is herself and the reality of the situation, and courage to face up to that reality. And in the end, that is all we have too: ourselves and reality. If we ask for meaning, for answers, then we must be prepared to do without a neat package that will flash up on the computer screen. Meaning is an ongoing process, not a book of answers, and it requires a deepening contact with reality – the reality of who we REALLY are, and the reality of what REALLY confronts us. And although we can get advice and feed-back along the way, in the end those two realities can be known only to us.

It is a lonely and frightening responsibility. If I put it another way, and say that the search for God must begin within ourselves, then the old programming will stir into protest – "God is out there; we can only find Him if we put self behind us." But is that true, or is it just another way of avoiding reality?

> . . . it is utter
> Terror and loneliness
> That drive a man to address the
>   Void as "Thou".

Talking to the computer, talking to the void – we might as well talk to ourselves. And perhaps that's just the point. We have to learn to talk to ourselves, or rather, to listen.

On holiday in Florence and saturated with great art, I staggered out of the rain into the Bargello Museum, mostly just to find somewhere to dry out, recover from a cultural overdose, and have a cup of coffee. But there, in a recess in the wall, stands Donatello's statue of St George. Not very saintly to look at – just a fairly ordinary young man – but the look on his face is riveting. He stares ahead of him, so that if you were fanciful you might look over your shoulder to make sure that the dragon wasn't coming up behind you. George stands alone, alert, facing the reality of what confronts him, with courage and determination.

We don't believe in dragons any more, just as we don't believe in alien space monsters. But courage – the courage to stand alone and face reality; do we believe in that? One last word before the main feature begins. We said that the word "religion" may have originated in the idea of tying together, and I wanted to use that in the sense of bringing together and trying to make a comprehensible bundle of all the bits and pieces that go to make up our lives. But Cicero thought the word came from somewhere else, that it comes from *relegere* – to read something over again. And perhaps that is important for us too. If we have a religious awareness of our lives, if we believe that what happens to us and to others really matters, then we will need to read over the story of our lives. What happens to us is not a random series of isolated incidents. We have to make a Gospel of our own lives. It is only by taking seriously what we see, think, feel, intuit, fear, love, hate, imagine, that we will ever get anywhere near the truth. And the truth, as the man said, will set us free.

1

The Prophet and The Donkey

After an overdose of culture in Florence, I escaped to the English sea-side, only to discover that they were in the middle of a heat wave. The only relief from the relentless sun was to hide in the theatre, but I found out that it isn't only in the cinema that alarming things can happen to you. . .

. . . It was a mistake to sit in the front row of the stalls for a half-empty matinée performance of "Holiday Suntime". Seated in solitary splendour, with a yawning void between me and the scattered few at the back of the theatre nursing their sunburn, I'd already been the subject of particular attentions from Ken Dodd and his tickling stick. But worse was to come. Onto the stage bounded a new comedy double act, eager to stake a place for themselves alongside other famous duos – Morecambe and Wise, Little and Large, Cannon and Ball, Laurel and Hardy . . . Much of their act involved the use of a "volunteer" from the audience, and as I was the only living soul within about a day's march of the stage, I suddenly found myself volunteered. For the next ten minutes I was sawn in half, thrust full of swords in a cabinet, made to disappear (but not, sad to say, in a puff of smoke), and used as a ventriloquist's dummy. Although the occasional whisper of "You all right mate?" proved my companions were human, I felt as if I'd been caught up in some weird religious rite. Like all these double acts, they each had a very distinct role to play: one wise, the other foolish, one funny, the other serious. A sort of comic battle raged around me, as the force of order and propriety struggled to keep up the façade of well-behaved normality, while his anarchic brother did everything he could to bring chaos.

I soon recovered from my ordeal, although I think I'll be more sensitive about where I put my hand next time I'm holding a ventriloquist's dummy. But it was an eye-opener to be caught up in the comic warfare that seems to be at the heart of so much comedy – the knowing adult against the foolish child. The audience had no doubt about whose side they were on. The more pompous and know-it-all the killjoy became, the more they longed for the fool he was treating with such contempt to give him his come-uppance. And in the end, as usually happens with these acts, it was the serious, moralizing "grown-up" who'd got it all wrong, and the childish prankster who'd been right all the time – if only his partner had taken him seriously and listened to him, he would have been saved an awful lot of chaos and humiliation.

There's another comedy double act which has been around a bit longer than my friends from Eastbourne. Actually, it's an animal act, and one that proves the old saying that if you want to keep your dignity on stage, you should never appear with children or animals. If you want to catch the act, you don't need to search through the Futurist Theatre, Scarborough, or the Winter Garden, Blackpool; it's in the Bible, in the book of Numbers.

The straight man of the act is called the prophet Balaam, and his partner is a donkey. Balaam is riding along on highly important prophetic business, when suddenly the donkey starts going off the rails – almost literally, as she veers off the road and into a field. The problem is that, as with most double acts, she knows something that the big important prophet doesn't: in this case, that their way is blocked by an angel standing in the way with a drawn sword in his hand. Balaam beats the ass, forcing her back onto the road. The path narrows, passing between two walls, and again the angel blocks the way, so the poor donkey presses herself up against the wall to avoid him. As with all good comedy acts, this means that the straight man gets it; Balaam's foot is squashed against the wall. And as with all good comedy acts, the straight man now proceeds to revenge himself on the comic; Balaam beats the donkey again. On they go, but this time the angel positions himself in a narrow place, where there's no turning to right or left. What can the donkey do but lie down – hopefully with the maximum amount of comic inconvenience to the prophet. He's furious, and starts beating her again, at which point she not unnaturally asks him, "What have I done to deserve three beatings?" The archetypal straight man, Balaam replies, "Because you've made a fool of me", and with a violence worthy of Oliver Hardy when Stan has done his worst, "I wish I had a sword with me, because I could KILL you for this. . . ." "Look here," says the donkey, "we've known each other all our lives and I've served you faithfully; have I ever let you down before?" Luckily, before things can degenerate into an "Oh yes you did", "Oh no I didn't" situation, with all the kids in the audience yelling "BEHIND YOU . . . THERE'S AN ANGEL BEHIND YOU . . .", the angel himself takes a hand. Or rather, God finally opens Balaam's eyes so that he can see for himself the heavily armed angel blocking his passage.

It's always one of the best bits when the pompous straight man, trying to exercise his authority, comes up against a figure of real authority, and I imagine an angel outranks even a Keystone Cop or the Sheriff of Nottingham. Balaam falls on his face, begging for mercy. It turns out that he owes his life to the donkey. If she hadn't seen the angel, and put up with three beatings to avoid him, then the angel would have killed Balaam, and let the donkey live. "I've been a fool", says Balaam. (Or, as this is the Bible after all, "I have sinned".)

Now with most comedy, you can take it or leave it — unless, of course, you get dragged up on stage to take part. But I have an uneasy feeling that with the comic duo of Balaam and the Ass, we have no option — we have been dragged up onto the stage; indeed, our whole lives are spent locked in the middle of the warfare between prophet and donkey. Unfortunately, once you're involved in the workings of a comedy act, you realize that it isn't at all funny: it's deadly serious and extremely hard work. No wonder the dying actor Kean, when asked how he felt, replied, "Dying is easy . . . comedy is difficult."

But how are we involved? Perhaps it would be easier to ask how are we not involved, because the struggle involves every area of our lives. It is, quite simply, about truth. It is about trying to find out what is most real and most true in our lives; all those simple and sneered at questions which we jokily associate with adolescence, when the truth is that we try to forget them by keeping as busy as possible, and it's only at times of growth or change or sudden stillness that they come rushing back again. Questions like (forgive me, you'll probably laugh, "Oh I know the answer to that one!") "Who am I?", "Why am I?", "Where am I?", "What does it all mean?", "Is there any way that I can possibly make sense out of this whole bewildering business, or do I just have to blunder on?"

Thomas Merton spoke about us belonging to a "perplexed and struggling race". We know the things that should matter to us . . . the first kiss, marriage, promotion, children, death . . . but somehow there's an awful lot of confusion in between, and after some of these so-called high spots, we may well wonder what all the fuss has been about. All that effort, all that expectation, all that strain, has gone into . . . what? And do we feel any more alive because of it? Perhaps we begin to ask ourselves, "What, if anything, does all this mean?"

The easiest thing to do with a question like that is to find an expert who will provide us with a half-convincing answer. But it may be that the only experts who will really be able to help us are the comedy duo, having their private battle inside us. Perhaps we should try to listen to what they are saying. Perhaps the time has come to start eavesdropping on their conversation.

For a start, you might say that the prophet represents a certain sort of religion, and the donkey stands for the average man or woman in the street. I hope it won't confuse matters here to introduce the figure of Procrustes. He was a robber who used to tie his victims down onto a bed. If they were too short to fit the bed exactly, he would stretch them until they fitted; if they were too long, he would cut pieces off them. Unfortunately, not many of his customers survived the fittings. And perhaps the mind of the prophet is a bit like Procrustes' bed. God, reality, meaning, experience – and in this case, another person's experience – can only be accepted if they fit exactly into his terms. Of course the donkey can't see an angel, because it's only a stupid animal getting on with its work. If there's anything important to be seen, then who else would see it but a highly important prophet? Unless what you say, what you think or what you feel fits exactly into a preconceived pattern, it will be censored or expanded until it can neatly pop into place.

When angels crop up in stories like this, they actually stand for God. In much the same way that the Jews wouldn't name God, out of respect, so they tended to say "the angel of the Lord" instead of God Himself. It's the same when Jacob wrestles with the "angel" – his adversary is really God. So what the prophet is actually guilty of is being so blind, so tied up in his own closed mind, that even when everything grinds to a halt, he still can't see God before his very eyes. But the donkey can see.

Perhaps a warning from this story is that prophets, or the

organized religion that they stand for, may be guilty of a serious con-trick. "God", they tell us, "is here, or there, or blue, pink, or green." More dangerously, they don't just tell us what we ought to think about God; they tell us what we ought to think about our own lives. The donkey stopped because she knew her way was barred; and, what's more, she knew who it was in the way. The prophet beats her to force her on her way – she must obey the one who knows.

I'm always fascinated by people's reactions when they step into a church, for perhaps one of the very few occasions in their lives. You can get so used to these strange and sometimes beautiful buildings, that you forget that for many of the 95 per cent or so of the population who never set foot inside, they feel strange, hollow, lifeless, threatening; somewhere completely alien from everything that matters to them in their lives. And sometimes the culture clash can be very comic. I had to take a funeral once, where most of the mourners arrived in an extremely happy state. They subsided quietly enough into the pews, but I hadn't got very far into the service when from the back of the chapel, and gradually increasing in volume as the other mourners joined in, came the familiar strains of "Should auld acquaintance be forgot, And never brought to min'. . . ." In a short time a battle had developed between the outraged Anglican parson, my voice rising to a banshee wail of Oxford vowels as I tried to punch home my sponsor's message, and the free-spirits of the congregation, who had at last found a way of expressing their grief that meant something to them. If I'd been a little wiser, and a little less on my clerical dignity, I think I should have gone down and joined them, so that we could all link hands and sing the thing properly. After all, are the sentiments so very different?

My problem in the chapel was partly one of language. You don't have to be a very sensitive cleric to realize that the bulk of the words, phrases and concepts which seem as commonplace to us as a shopping list, are actually an alien tongue to the outsider. Words like "redemption", "salvation", "resurrection" or "Holy Spirit", make about as much sense to the uninitiated as they would if I were to stand up, robed and serious, and recite "To be or not to be" in Esperanto.

The mistake is to assume that because people don't share a language, they won't understand or have experienced the basic concepts behind the words. I saw myself as the guardian of a truth, Rome standing firm against the Goths and Vandals, when perhaps the truth is more likely to be that I had absolutely no idea of what was going on in that chapel, or of the thoughts, feelings, emotions involved. I was the prophet trying to beat the congregation into submission, and make them listen to MY words, MY language, force them to see MY God . . . when all the time, they could see perfectly clearly what they needed to see, and I was too proud to get down and listen to them.

If we take the lesson of the donkey and the prophet seriously, then it has many implications for our ideas about religion. If the person who assumes that he is the expert on God, and who is going about his religious business, is the very person who can't see God, then we're entitled to ask if there's any reason why we should believe what he tells us . . . why we shouldn't instead listen to what the voice of our own experience is telling us. Maybe the people to pay attention to are the donkeys – the ones who get on with living their lives, and find God confronting them in the ordinary, everyday business of living. Maybe we need to pay attention to our own lives as they really are, not as we'd like to pretend they are or as we feel some external prophet would like them to be.

Because it isn't just in matters religious that we surrender authority. The new priestly hierarchy, the scientists and their creeds, now command our devotion and obedience.

Just as we obediently used to believe that religious talk was about some objective reality that really was there, if only we could see it, so now we gamely repeat the scientific creeds, with about as much comprehension as we had for the Latin Mass. Now this is not to attack science; I'm not trying to set it up as an Aunt Sally so that I can knock it down in two superficial paragraphs and replace it with some good old-time religion. What I am setting up as an Aunt Sally, or at least sending off danger signals about, is the sort of fatalistic and lazy idolatry with which we regard the scientific world view. Science has brought fantastic benefit to the world. (Yes, all right, but we'll leave pollution, nuclear weapons, chemical and biological warfare, etc., out for the moment.) You only have to look at the change, for example, in the medical textbooks, from my grandfather's time to now, to see how very much that was deadly or incurable, and that caused untold suffering, has actually been made a thing of the past. But we somehow assume that science KNOWS . . . that it has unlocked the secrets of the universe. Tosh!

The scientific prophet riding the donkey may be incredibly wise, incredibly gifted, incredibly knowledgeable, but he or she is still human. Do we somehow believe that these people are not subject to the same emotions as we are, the same drives, the same passions? Is any human being capable of making a purely objective choice about anything, unswayed by all those conscious and unconcious forces that sweep us around like the tide? Can you honestly say, in any given situation, if you stop to think about what you have done, that you completely understand what made you act? Of course, we can all come up with a long list of motives and intentions, most of which, if true, should lead to the instant sprouting of angelic wings, but do conscious word and actual deed really measure up? Scientific truth is relative and metaphoric. Who knows what drives the scientist to look in a particular area? And when he is there, his thoughts are constrained by the governing images, the mythology, within which he works. "Physics is an attempt conceptually to grasp reality as it is thought", said Einstein. If it is truth, it is symbolic truth. Einstein again: "Atomic theory should be viewed more as a visualizing symbol than as knowledge concerning the factual construction of matter."

Despite the mad scientist of Hollywood fame, we have invented a myth about a new generation of prophets whose thoughts and actions are controlled purely by reason. Now that religion has gone down the plug-hole, we need new gods to reassure us; a new cosmic Mummy and Daddy who will look after us and make sure that everything turns out all right in the end. And yet these prophets can be just as narrow-minded as Balaam. Try getting a scientist to think in terms outside his own particular theology, or the particular theoretical concepts by which he lives and moves and has his being. The poor consumer, or rather the poor mass of people on whose backs these experts ride, can only gratefully accept the crumbs. And yet the whole business is riddled with mythology. We still believe that science has spelled out for us objective and immutable truths about existence, when in reality there can be very few areas which are subject to total agreement amongst the experts, and no areas at all which are not subject to that most basic scientific truth of all – that there is no such thing as absolute objectivity. "What we establish mathematically is 'objective fact' only in small part," wrote Heisenberg, "in larger part it is a survey of possibilities." Neither you, the person observing, can stand outside the limitations of your own being; nor it, the thing observed, can be known in any other terms except those of being under observation: an object, whose reality may or may not correspond with the way it is seen to behave when under scrutiny.

You could draw up a long list of other prophets, none of

whom would stand up to much scrutiny. Medicine for one, or politics, or the State. So much of our lives now seems to depend on experts, and we become increasingly passive as we wait for the right expert to come and make things better. And all will be well, maybe, if the prophet is prepared to enter into a constructive dialogue with the donkey – but how often does that happen? The danger of prophets/experts is that they may be too constrained by their own fantasies/theories to be able to see or hear what is really before their eyes. And they have all the advantages; language for one.

Although the donkey is finally forced into speech by Balaam's cruelty, she still doesn't seem able to tell him exactly what the matter is. All she can do is to register a protest, and hint that if Balaam were bright enough he'd cotton on to the fact that something must be wrong for her to behave so unusually. She knows something that he doesn't, but he cannot learn from her or share her experience.

And there lies the problem. The experts have all the words. The whole of life and experience can be captured and pinned down in words. A butterfly flies over the long grass, the sun catching the dancing colours of its wings. A quick swoop of the net, and it is caught, and then quickly into the specimen jar where it is smothered. Finally, back home to the collection. A large pin impales the dead and fraying body onto a card. Neatly written under the corpse come the words which name it, and yet which were also its death sentence: Nymphalis Pyrameis.

In much the same way, you might say that all doctrine and religious formulae are parasitic upon the original experience. I'm going to get into trouble if I call Jesus a butterfly, but what was primary and true and real was His life as He experienced it, and as those around Him shared it. But the moment you start trying to put down in words what you think that experience meant, you move into a different mode of being. The analytic, intellectual mind starts forcing what was subjective, sensed, felt, experienced, into the mould of words. And with words come concepts and patterns of thought. Not only are the words parasitic upon the original experience, but they may change its very meaning in order to fit it into our neat philosophic patterns. The butterfly is impaled, and slowly turns to dust, until all that is left is the original label. At the expense of the odd arm or leg or head, Procrustes fits another victim onto his bed.

We need words; we'd die without them. But the message of the donkey is to insist that we should take our experience seriously – even, that language just isn't capable of taking true account of what matters in our lives. Think about some experience in your life that really moved you. Have you kept it to yourself, or have you shared it with others? Perhaps it was something quite simple, like a sunset or watching a baby. Perhaps it was more complex, like watching someone you love walking towards you. Perhaps it was death or marriage or birth. But if it is something that you have talked about a lot, is there a sense in which it has become a story for you – something which you relate, but which seems to lose more and more of its reality? Or, if you love someone, can you describe them to me in a few sentences? And even if you do that, will I still be any nearer understanding why you love that person, or you any nearer expressing what this love means to you? And is there a sense of disappointment, as if something very precious has been made to sound banal?

When I heard the learn'd astronomer,
When the proofs, the figures, were
   ranged in columns before me,
When I was shown the charts and
   diagrams, to add, divide, and
   measure them,
When I sitting heard the astronomer
   where he lectured with much
   applause in the lecture room,
How soon unaccountable I became
   tired and sick,
Till rising and gliding out I wander'd
   off by myself,
In the mystical moist night-air, and
   from time to time,
Look'd up in perfect silence at the stars.

Walt Whitman

2

Male and Female He Created

So far, we have been looking at the prophet as if he always came from outside ourselves. But that knowing, superior voice is there inside us too; given his head, he could lead us to destruction.

If that sounds almost heretical, perhaps it's because the image of a man mounted on an animal is quite a good picture of the way we see ourselves. Man, upright, rational, an immortal soul, is somehow involved in an embarrassing relationship with something animal – our bodies. And just as donkeys defecate and smell and get sexy, so do we; but somehow we'd like to feel that part of ourselves rises above the experience. It's the old religious thing again . . . matter bad, evil, naughty (but nice): Spirit clean, pure, uncorrupted and so on. In its most extreme form, you have sects whose chapels are built without windows so that when the good people are at prayer, they will not be distracted by being able to see the sinful world outside. And included in being sinful, of course, are not just the people outside, but trees, clouds, sunlight, birds – all created, all made of matter, all bad.

And so we tend to think of ourselves as minds or spirits imprisoned in the flesh. Our bodies can seem almost external to ourselves, or we think "I have a body", in much the same way that we might say "I have a car" or "I have a house". It feels very hard to say "I am my body", but isn't that what is actually true? Every single experience in our lives is physical, because it is with our bodies that we do the experiencing. But just as the prophet likes to ride the donkey, to own it, to give it orders, to beat it; so our egos look down on our bodies, in much the same way that our eyes look down on our bodies, assessing them from the outside.

The prophet wants to control and own the donkey; we treat our bodies as so much meat. Meat to be tanned or tenderized; meat to be de-fatted or re-shaped with new muscle; meat to be trained for sexual gymnastics; meat to look good in the shop window. Meat to carry us where we want to go, and that we will ignore until suddenly it lies down under us, or crushes our foot against a wall. This isn't the place to talk about holistic medicine, but that's where one of the biggest prophetic bluffs is beginning to be called. For so long we've been taught to think of medicine in a mechanical way: I have a body; one of the components has gone wrong; I have called the expert; he will fix it for me. But suddenly we're beginning to see that you can't separate mind, body and emotions. The whole person is involved. The easiest and least dramatic example would be the way it was discovered a fashion model developed an unusual and unsightly rash on her face at a time when she badly needed, emotionally, to get away from her work; ditto a boxer, with a rash all over his torso; and ditto a surgeon with a painful rash on his hands. To put it crudely, you might say that there is something inside us which actually gives permission to our bodies to be ill. We all carry around the cold germ at all times; what makes us decide when and where we are going to develop a cold?

Without the donkey to keep him in his place, the prophet can imagine himself all-seeing, all-knowing, even, most dangerously, all-powerful. Luckily, the donkey can strike back, sometimes in ways very similar to crushing her rider's foot against a wall. The body can come up with some very symbolic illnesses – back-pain for one. Quite often you may find that the person who is struggling to carry too much in their life – too much emotion, too much responsibility – will suddenly be crippled by back trouble. And they can either soldier on, with experts coming in to mend the machine, or they can have the sense to stop and listen to what the donkey is telling them.

Perhaps it is no surprise that it should be a she-donkey. To use the Jungian "mythology", you might say that the prophet is the male principle, all to do with the will, reason, the power of the conscious mind; striving, assertive, and, without the feminine principle to balance it, about as deadly to itself and others as a Sherman tank. Sooner or later, left to its own devices, it will be in confrontation with an angel with a drawn sword. The donkey is different. The feminine principle is darker, less obvious, to do with all those parts of the personality that cannot be tied down so easily: moods, emotions, reactions rather than actions. It cannot be directly controlled by the will. Warmth, compassion, receptivity, gentleness – of all Christ's strengths, surely the strongest was his weakness, and his sympathy and understanding for the weakness of others. It is in the womb of Mary that God's ultimate statement of love is prepared.

Perhaps I should hurry to explain, in case it isn't clear already, that I'm not talking about the difference between men and women. I said before that the prophet and the donkey are a comedy act inside all of us, men and women alike. We all share the male and the female principles; it is when we won't listen to them, or when we emphasize one at the expense of the other, that we run into trouble. If the donkey doesn't have the prophet, she may wander off into the fields and never be seen again. If the prophet doesn't have the donkey, his blind will may drive him to try to run over God.

The classical myths understand all about this. Hercules, butchest of all the heroes, struggles through task after task asserting his invincible male strength. But just as even the strongest man may find himself bewildered by his inability to control his moods and emotions, so Hercules' constant self-assertive struggle leads not to happiness, but to madness. Everything starts to go wrong in his life, and in despair he goes to the Delphic oracle for help. But he is not yet ready to learn from a woman, and his male pride revolts at this feminine intrusion into his life. More madness and more trouble follow, and he is almost caught up in warfare with the gods. At last the answer comes; the only way out for Hercules is for him to be sold as a slave to a woman. For three years, he serves Queen Omphale. She beats him and ridicules him, and wears his armour, whilst he sits sewing with her female servants, dressed as a woman. Only after this is he restored to harmony, and in the end he marries Omphale.

Real strength, real wholeness, real autonomy, come when the two principles are in harmony together. So Jewish philosophers would assert that Adam was "man on the right side and woman on the left side, but God has cloven him into two halves". And back to the classical myths for a warning about what happens when you ignore this need for wholeness. . . . Orpheus must be about the earliest model in our Western culture of the ascetic, other-worldy religious person. After the death of his wife, he shunned human company, especially that of women. In the end, the whole feminine side of life turns on him, and he is torn to pieces by the Maenads – the priestesses of Bacchus, caught up in the madness of the dance of life. We ignore the world of feeling, mood, image and fantasy at our peril.

This need for balance is a theme which runs through every religious tradition. And when the traditions ignore it, when they let the prophet have all the say, then it is no wonder that they shrivel up and wither for lack of nurture. At the risk of being superficial, can I briefly mention just a few examples? In Jewish tradition, the Sabbath is feminine. Work is put to one side, and the great emphasis is on family, relationship, comfort and ease. The whole of the Old Testament is full of feminine imagery: Israel as bride, and as slut, running after other lovers; the promised land, flowing with milk and honey. Or look at the figure of the Buddha. I remember standing bewildered in front of the great Buddha of Kamakura – everything he stood for seemed so alien to my (Christian) tradition, as I then perceived it. His figure is impassive, calm, waiting; almost pregnant with stillness. And physically, he is more like an ancient earth-mother than the sort of hyperactive, muscular saints of Michelangelo that we are used to. Heavy breasted, round bellied, he sits and waits. His eyes are closed, but his huge ears are open, receptive, ready to take in. He would not, you feel, be an asset in a rendition of "Onward Christian Soldiers".

And yet that stillness and receptivity is very much part of the Christian tradition. Perhaps the most explored theme, after the crucifixion, is that of the Annunciation. For centuries, artists and writers have sought to depict the scene. Simone Martini's painting of the Annunciation, in the Uffizi in Florence, shows a young girl looking with horror at the angel; as if to avoid what he has to ask, her whole body is twisted away from him. But in her openness to God, in her willingness to accept the mysterious and unknown which will grow inside her, lies her essential role in God's redemptive plan.

I've drawn up a long line of witnesses in support of the donkey and her representing to us the feminine. But in the end, perhaps one can put it most simply by saying that the religious moment, the openness to God, cannot and will not happen unless the feminine is full and free, waiting passively on God, waiting for the wound of love. As far as the things of God are concerned, the prophet is blind. His agenda is too full for him to find space for anything but his own wishes.

If you imagine the prophet riding along on the donkey, it is as if the whole centre of gravity is right at the top of the picture – in the prophet's head. Our danger is that we will see ourselves purely as mind and ego, the rational controllers of a mechanical enterprise. My body may be "mine", but it is still an object, an "it", something I possess – there is always the fantasy that the rider can dismount at any time. When God became flesh, it was in a place of rejection, amongst dumb animals. His first worshippers were religious outcasts; shepherds were considered unclean because of their closeness to all the noise and dirt and reality of animals. God forbid anything animal should be allowed to intrude into church. In a few days the Holy Family would be refugees, running for their lives, because the men of action, the planners, the rulers, were out for blood, as they sensed that things were slipping out of their control.

I'm going on and on about this, because it is a most central and vital part of our journey. We have got to accept that we are prophet AND donkey. We have got to take part in our own incarnation – actually to begin to accept and experience the fact of being: being present here and now, the warmth and pleasure and ease and reality of our feelings, sensations, moods. Male and female, the prophet and the donkey on their journey together, thought and feeling. If our religious quest is ruled by the ego, the one who wants to "have" knowledge and to be in control, then our place is in the court of King Herod. "God may be coming . . . Where? When? Why?" – take action, plan, stay in control, keep on top of the situation. Or have we the courage to go back to the place that people avoid – the stable of our own messy, tired, rejected humanity, and there quietly, with the dumb animals, wait for new birth, wait for the approach of God?

3

Computer Games

"It has been said," he began at length, withdrawing his eyes reluctantly from an unusually large insect upon the ceiling and addressing himself to the maiden, "that there are few situations in life that cannot be honourably settled, and without loss of time, either by suicide, a bag of gold, or by thrusting a despised antagonist over the edge of a precipice on a dark night."

Kai Lung's Golden Hours

If only it were that simple! There are two last antagonists who need looking at, and who can make the prophet particularly blind. As we cannot bribe them away, or ask them to do the decent thing, perhaps we can make them less powerful by exposing them to the light of day.

In a sense, we have met them already, but they deserve a closer look. One we can never escape, because it is bred into the bone. The other is a tight-fitting garment, woven around us by society. But where to begin?

Perhaps we ought to start with Dr Freud, that brilliant explorer and prophet, who dared to face and name the tragic forces at work in us. Freud likened the mind to an iceberg, where the small part showing above the water represents the region of consciousness, while the larger mass below the water represents the region of unconsciousness. And, of course, it is on the hidden ice below the water that the unsinkable ship *Titanic* tears out its innards.

It would be only fair to say that Freud's theories have been criticized because they were based on his work with troubled personalities. Perhaps if we treat what he has to tell us as another helpful mythology, we can learn from his insights, without having to say that this is the exact and only truth.

According to Freud, we have within us three major systems: the id, the ego, and the superego. The id represents those parts of the personality that we are born with: instincts, inherited potentials, and our physiological body processes. Within the id, there is a conflict between the life instincts, which are basically sexual, and the death instincts, which are our destructive and hostile impulses. The ego comes about as a sort of mediator between the basic drives of the id, seeking only for pleasure, and the reality of the outside world. The ego is guided by our intellect, and thinks, plans ahead, makes decisions and so on. The superego is made up of the social values that have been taught us by family, society and religion.

For Freud, these three elements are constantly at war. The id wants to have a good time, or beat a few people up – it is always seeking to express itself in the real world. If you imagine the personality as a house, then the id would be all the strange dark creatures in the basement, trying to force themselves up into the light of day. The superego would be the roof of the house, acting as a lid on what might emerge from the basement. But the main part of the house is the ego, trying to get through daily life and the pressures of reality. The greater the weight of the roof (presumably made up of slates with "good boy", "bad boy", "naughty", "obey", "sin" and so on written on them) the greater the pressure on the ego, so that the personality has very little control in its relations with the real world. And the door to the basement is sealed tight shut – and perhaps liable to explode open one day in a killing spree, or an affair with the secretary.

Or it could be that the roof is a very patchy affair. Without that downward pressure, all the impulses from the basement can be acted upon without any great concern for their impact on others or on society.

So what would the ideal house be like? Somehow the person living mainly in the centre of the house could still be in touch with the other parts. He or she could go down into the basement, maybe have a playroom there, and also be able to throw out some of its lumber, like repressed conflicts from childhood. He or she would also be more aware of some of the creatures that might be lurking there. And he/she could climb up onto the roof and examine the tiles – perhaps in some places there is too great a weight of them, so the ones that are no longer needed can be disposed of, or perhaps there are some holes that need patching.

If you ask what sort of house the prophet might live in, then I think the danger is that he might live in a house with a massive roof; so massive, indeed, that the light of day can hardly filter into the rooms. Religion would be like a great cover thrown over the place, and the poor prophet would be left alone, a ghostly figure – hardly human – in a world of cobwebs and shadows.

Of course, religion could be the force that flings back the shutters and lets in the light of reality. But perhaps the danger Freud is hinting at, is that religion, as it is commonly perceived, appeals precisely because it filters out reality.

This theme extends into the research that has been done on what is called the Authoritarian Personality. Studying the personalities of people who were highly prejudiced, researchers found that there is a very definite personality structure with distinct traits. These traits include a very conventionalized social conformity, a strong puritanical conscience, admiration of power and strength, belief in severe punishment, worry about status, repressed sexuality, a rigidly black-and-white style of thinking, a tendency to distrust others, and a tendency to see the world as evil and dangerous. I'm not sure how many different theologies there are in the world which would slot very neatly into some, or all, of those categories, but I fear that we might find an alarming number. One trait which I have not mentioned is that there is a repressed hostility towards the parents, and a deep ambivalence about social norms and the authorities who enforce them.

In many ways, there is a religion which shows the same kind of ambivalence. God is all-powerful, His condemnation of sinners total. Religion becomes a desperate scurrying around to keep Him at a distance, usually by placating Him with the appropriate sacrifices, and by sticking rigidly to the book of rules. Whether or not we can actually love such a tyrant is another question.

Another way of looking at personality, is to see it as it responds to social and economic pressures. Reisman talks of three basic directions in personality development, all of which are found in us to a greater or lesser degree. The first is "Tradition-Directed", where personality is largely determined by all the demands, customs, beliefs and attitudes of a person's particular social group – especially the family. In a sense, it is an enormously secure life, with the burden of decision-making taken away from the individual. A man will follow in his father's footsteps, perhaps taking over the same job. He will marry within his own social group, and his life will be governed by the rules and pressures of that group. In the industrialized West, it is a dying way of life, but perhaps still to be found in some rural areas and in areas of high unemployment, where the community has stayed but the industry has died or moved on. Whether or not you believe, or what you believe, will depend on what the group does or does not believe. You might say that such a person's decision-making process is outside them – it belongs to the group.

The second direction of personality is "Inner-Directed", where the superego determines the personality. All the demands, customs and beliefs of the individual's social group have been internalized, to provide a constant set of answers in a rapidly changing and highly complex world. The voice of conscience is particularly strong, and failure to obey it leads to intense feelings of guilt. To go back to the spaceship, it is as if the controls were permanently locked on to a computer programme that was initiated by the parents at the start of the journey. Getting off course leads to guilt; seeing others off course leads to anger. And following such a programme may take the ship to where others want it to go, but it probably won't take the individual to the place where he or she really wants to go.

At the core of the problem is the belief that one's real self is an unreliable guide, so instead of following the real self, one follows an inflexible moral code or a stringent set of ideals which one believes one must conform to. In the movie, following the computer led to destruction by the monster. In real life, it may lead to a pattern of life that is admired by others, but the real needs of the particular real person are ignored, leading to a growing sense of being thwarted. Life becomes grey; an endless succession of hurdles.

The tradition-directed personality finds stability by staying at home; the inner-directed by remaining in familiar surroundings or by following the programming of his conscience when in new situations. The third group are "Other-Directed", and find their stability by being able to adapt rapidly to change. The personality is largely determined by parents and social group, but the number and kind of influencing groups is much larger. Quickly able to adapt to new situations, new demands, customs or beliefs, the whole emphasis of his/her parental conditioning was not on a rigid code of behaviour but on the skills necessary for getting on successfully with others.

Social approval is all, for the other-directed personality, and if it doesn't come, then anxiety sets in. A good mixer, popular, well adjusted (seemingly), he or she is almost bound to win social approval; this is, after all, still the age of "how to win friends and influence people".

But there is a price for all this popularity, and it is that success has been bought at the price of ignoring or denying what he/she really feels as an individual. Gradually, it may become more and more difficult to establish close relationships. Even your husband or wife may be just another acquaintance that you have to please. Would they accept you if they knew what you were really thinking?

Each of us contains a cocktail made up of these three ingredients. All of us have been brought up by people older than ourselves, and, like it or not, their programmes will always be locked inside us. And all of us respond, to a greater or lesser extent, to the expectations of those around us. And we have tribal voices inside us too; expert politicians or propagandists can be very skilful at setting those tapes running.

But there is another direction we can take. Unfortunately, it involves an act of faith on our part. When we have to choose what to do about something, we might rely on a code of action laid down by some group, or on the judgement of others (be they husband, friends, mother or Claire Rayner), or on the way we have behaved in the past. Or else, we might rely on ourselves. It sounds simple, but it actually involves learning to trust ourselves and being open to the full reality of the situation.

Put like that, it sounds so simplistic. Of course we trust ourselves! But my fear is that, far from being easy, such trust involves an act of faith which is far more complex than that demanded by any religion. All our programming, the voices of parents, culture, education, the political and economic system, tends to provide a set of answers which it is extremely painful to ignore. From these voices, which have been drilling us from the moment of birth, we learn: who we are (or who others think we ought to be), what is important to us (or what others think we ought to value), how to satisfy certain needs, some ways to solve problems, and some ways to handle our feelings.

All of this is a product of our past. We can also let it be the architect of our present and future – all that we need to do is obediently to follow our programming. There is a book by William Golding, called *Lord of the Flies*, which could almost be the Bible of this approach. It's a horrific story of a group of small boys, marooned on an island. The civilized veneer of their behaviour is quickly stripped away, until they become bloodthirsty and vicious savages. This, you feel, is what humanity would really be like, without the restraints of law and order, and the threat of punishment.

Or would it? And that's where the act of faith comes in. At base, it's something to do with whether one believes that humanity is essentially good or bad; whether you and I can trust ourselves.

And perhaps the unthinking answer comes back, "Yes, of course I can trust myself", but hanging unspoken in the air lie a little stream of "ifs . . . buts . . . althoughs . . ."

I was sitting in a train, on my way to give a talk to some gathering. As typecasting in public speakers is almost as inevitable as it is for actors, the subject of the talk was almost certainly something to do with freedom, the need for openness of vision, and so on. I was sharing the compartment with two sweet little old ladies, and although I was hoping fervently that we wouldn't get into conversation, they seemed at least to guarantee a peaceful and uneventful journey. How wrong could I be? At the next stop, horror of horrors, three punk-rockers scrambled into the compartment. Their clothes were filthy, and seemed to be held together only with the help of lashings of safety pins, lengths of chain and, from the look of it, rust. Their Mohican haircuts would have made a lavatory brush manufacturer pale with envy. They were noisy, covered with tattoos, and appeared to have brought a lifetime's supply of canned beer with them.

You can't work for the Church of England for long, without realizing that it has cornered the market in sweet little old ladies. Battle plans were forming in my mind as I coolly assessed the situation. Should I jump off the train, and leave the little old ladies to their fate? (First choice.) Should I shoulder the responsibility vested in me by the church, and defend its property – presumably by keeping these savages at bay until the next stop, and then shepherding my charges safely into another compartment? (Last choice.) Should I rip off my dog-collar, and pretend to be another punk in disguise? (About third choice.) Would the punks believe me, if I claimed to be a master of Kung Fu?

In the end, the decision was taken out of my hands. I was so caught up in trying to work out how to deal with these alien intruders, that I didn't notice them getting into conversation with the old ladies. It was only the fizzing noise of a can of Pepsi being opened, that brought me back to reality. The punks were sharing their picnic lunch with the old ladies, and the five of them were having an animated chat about the beauties of the countryside through which we were passing.

The little old ladies, whom I had so patronizingly regarded as church property, had passed the test of reality with flying colours. For the rest of the journey I sat and seethed with shame and anger at myself, as five thoroughly nice people got on with the job of being loving, real human beings, and all my neat little preconceptions, the moulds into which I would have liked to fit them, lay in pieces around me. Of all the people in that compartment, I was the one without vision or humanity. Instead of seeing people, I had just seen types who fitted into my lazy mental categories – "little old lady", "social outcast"; in fact, I had been so preoccupied with keeping up my defensive barriers, that I hadn't even noticed the beauty of the scenery until one of the punks mentioned it.

It's a silly example – I'm afraid I could draw up a very long list of others which are equally silly. But what I'm trying to get at is the fact that it is so intensely hard for us to see clearly, really to see what is happening. It is the difficult and painful lesson we have to learn from psychology; that the past modifies how we understand the present. In a sense, nothing can change that. I said at the beginning of this chapter that our conditioning is bred into the bone. Before we have even stopped playing with our teddy bears, the tapes have been locked into place in our minds.

And yet there is a way forward. If we can accept the reality of who we are – and that includes the reality of our conditioning – then we can still make genuine choices. And that includes the choice of ignoring the voice that comes from the computer – or rather, of assessing what it has to say in the light of reality.

I began with Freud, and the picture he gives us of ourselves. Perhaps it seemed a dark picture, as if we are the victims of a dark warfare going on within us. And it is certainly true that our biology can enslave us. We live between two dangerous poles, two possible sources of human slavery. A body can immobilize itself through the search for gratification; when pleasure is the greatest goal society can offer, we drive ourselves mad in its pursuit. Society can also imprison us for its own ends; in the name of freedom, it can put people into concentration camps. Each of us lives somewhere between these two poles, and somewhere between these two poles lies the precious ground that we must fight for: the integrity of the human personality – something so important, that every culture stands under judgement against it, every way of life is put to question.

I want to end this section with another picture of the way we are. In a sense, it brings together all that we have been looking at.

Transactional analysis is a highly sophisticated way of looking at human development and interaction. Its "mythology" sees us as being made up of three ego-states, each of which contains an interlinked system of feeling, thinking and behaviour. These ego-states are called Parent, Adult and Child, and usually we can only operate in one of these at any one time. The Parent and Child states have usually been largely formed by the time we are eight. The Parent develops from what we have been taught by our actual parents and by other significant adults – not just from what they said, but from what we saw them being and doing. Rather like an automatic pilot, the Parent in us will respond immediately and automatically to childlike behaviour, and to situations where we feel we have to take charge.

You can hear the Parent tape playing in yourself, or in others, when the voice becomes confident, commanding or demanding; it establishes rules of conduct, sets limits, enforces the rules, teaches manners, rewards and punishes. Even if it isn't actually the case, the Parent is convinced that it knows what is correct and ethical. The Parent also supports and helps others by reassuring them and doing things for them, and it stands up for the weak and ignorant. It likes to rescue people, even if their best interests would be served by being allowed to find their own answers.

The Child ego-state contains a person's basic desires and needs, and recordings of the world of experiences he or she felt as a child. It has two parts: the natural or spontaneous child, naturally feeling about and acting upon its needs, desires and impulses; and the adapted child – the part that has had to learn strategies for living with the all-powerful adults it depends upon. The natural child is affectionate, fun-loving, creative, greedy, impulsive, sensuous, spontaneous, unashamed and loving. The adapted child has learnt to comply or to rebel. If someone starts to use the Parental tone of voice to us, we can latch straight into the feelings and behaviour we had as children − that strange and inappropriate "sinking feeling", for instance, when we are dressed down by a superior; or the way we can harbour a grudge, or sulk or procrastinate. Or else, the way we can rush up to someone, wagging our tails, looking for approval or protection or permission. There is even the sinking feeling of realizing, after years of being able to go to the top for approval or for confirmation of what we are doing, that suddenly we ourselves *are* the people at the top; there is no higher authority. We are the grown-ups now! It was Pope John XXIII who said, "It often happens that I wake at night and begin to think about a serious problem and decide I must tell the Pope about it. Then I wake up completely and remember that I *am* the Pope."

Some people make a very good living out of staying almost permanently in their adapted child. Wherever there is something to rebel about, be sure that they will be there. Even as they approach pensionable age, they will be there, complaining about "Them".

And between these two ego-states lies the Adult − the reality principle. It observes, assesses, processes all the data coming in to it. In the light of reality, it can edit the old recordings made by Parent or Child.

Like the Freudian "house", all will be well if there is a balance between the different parts, if someone can be in touch with their Parent, their Adult and their Child. Unfortunately, life isn't that easy. When we are little, the adults, those who have power over us, can have an almost magical effect on us. It is when Sleeping Beauty is a baby that the spells are cast over her; spells that will imprison her at the first sign of adulthood. And "spells" is not too dramatic a word. We do have spells cast over us by the commands of our parents, and the personalities THEY attribute to us. From how early on in your life can you remember hearing commands like "Grow up", "Don't be childish", "Be responsible"? (i.e., you have no right to childhood with all its tumult, messiness and fun). Or commands like "Big boys don't cry", "Girls shouldn't fight", "Always be friendly, never say no, never show your anger, never be hostile . . .", "Don't touch yourself there, that's dirty."

And the attributions, usually made in the presence of others, telling us who or what we really are . . . "Richard's a big, tough kid", "Angela's lazy and not very clever, but she's going to be a beauty", "the trouble with him is he's spoiled", "of course, we always really wanted to have a son . . ." It was Pascal who said, "Man is so made that by continually telling him he is a fool, he believes it, and by continually telling it to himself he makes himself believe it." When we are children, we are uniquely vulnerable to these messages, spoken or unspoken.

And no one can blame the parents, because they're only playing the tapes programmed into them by their parents. But perhaps we learn that our emotional life doesn't really count; it is only our performance and behaviour that are recognized. And from that, we learn not to value ourselves for what we are or what we feel, but only for what we do.

In other words, perhaps a lot of us come out of the system able only to function in our Parent and Adult states. We may thrive on looking after those weaker than ourselves, and perhaps feel expert in knowing what is good for others. Perhaps, too, we pride ourselves on our objectivity, our ability to solve problems, our fund of factual knowledge. Mr and Mrs Darling keep secure and pompous house, whilst outside in the darkness, Peter Pan flies unseen and unheard. In other words, this one-up position of right and strength, knowing what is best for ourselves and others, is bought at the cost of blocking out the Child in us. The world of chaos, strong feelings, spontaneity and vulnerability – the whole creative part of our personalities – is kept firmly locked away.

In its most extreme form, you can see this at work in the strains in the medical profession. This isn't just the old truism that doctors make bad patients – although that is certainly something that finds an echo in the other helping professions; people who almost define themselves by being The Helper, the strong partner in a relationship, find it extremely hard to allow themselves to lose control, to be weak, to be cared for in their turn.

But the problem goes deeper than that. The rate of suicide amongst doctors is at least double that of the rest of the population. The rate of drug abuse and marital breakdown is similarly high. Harder to measure, but probably equally significant, are the number of marriages that have atrophied.

The public face, of course, remains good. Families and colleagues, for example, conceal the rate of alcoholism amongst doctors. And who dares mention the crisis in clergy marriages? Wife-beating in the vicarage – surely not possible, is it?

I said this was the extreme form, but the pattern is there for all "carers": spending their lives looking after weakness in others, they (we) are incapable of acknowledging or allowing themselves (ourselves) to have those same weaknesses.

I speak particularly as a Christian. We spend hours and hours praying for others "less fortunate than ourselves". Our knees aching, our brains reeling, we try to care as endless lists of names and places are unfolded before us. And at the end of the pray, what have we achieved? The ironic fact is that other groups, who make far fewer claims to expertise or concern about human suffering, just get on with the job, and probably do it far more effectively.

We talk endlessly about love – love God, love neighbour,

love the people of Pago Pago, even, horror of horrors, love that rat-faced little man in the next pew who bores you to tears over coffee after the service, unless you can manage to escape from church quickly enough and avoid the vicar's reproachful gaze. (The vicar's VERY reproachful gaze, because if he can't intimidate you into dealing with the rat-faced bore, he may just have to do it himself . . .)

And the quality of our love is? Well, perhaps the guilt we feel is a measure of the fact that we know we don't really love anybody very much. We can rescue them (Poor Mrs So and So, such a shame, of course I'd be delighted to take her on the outing, as long as she doesn't embarrass everyone by crying about her husband – really, she should have more self-control), or we can convert them, or pat them on the head, or pray for them; but we can't love them, because that would mean getting involved. And there's nothing more unsettling than getting involved with another human being. People are so messy. They have emotions; they behave differently to the way we like or expect; their pain is unpleasant, ugly and disturbing; their thoughts may be different to ours. No wonder we prefer dogs and cats.

Oh, of course we can be NICE to people; we can be endlessly nice, as the smile congeals on our faces, and we stare at them, hoping they'll be nice in return. But somehow it is so difficult to be genuinely interested in them, to make the effort really to listen to what they are saying, to accept them as they really are, without wishing we could adjust them to suit our taste. Perhaps you have heard that clarion call of disaster before a marriage, "I'll soon break him/her of that little habit, after we're married . . ." And perhaps they will, if they manage to break their partner in the process.

If the Child in us is so blocked off that we cannot hear it, then we only have the option of meeting people through the eyes of our Adult and Parent. That means that the only people we can feel warmly about – if we are capable of feeling warmly about anything except our dislike of weirdos – are people who meet our Parental approval. PLU – people like us.

And this begins with our very attitude to ourselves. The only parts of ourselves that we like to think about or acknowledge, are the parts that we have been trained to think are acceptable – the part that succeeds, that makes a good marriage, that owns a house, that votes for the right party, that goes to church, that doesn't get depressed or worried or break down and cry.

So, naturally, we like to spend our time with people like ourselves, as long as they don't let the side down by getting depressed or worried or crying. People who are truthful about their emotions can be extremely embarrassing.

A few years ago, I was taken by some kind friends to stay at a hugely luxurious hotel: the sort where you feel guilty every time the hall-porter looks at you, in case you have made a mark on the deep-pile carpet. The hotel was set on a cliff top, and you could lie around the swimming pool, shaded by palm trees, watching the ocean far below, and the ships'coming and going in the distant harbour. It was idyllic.

The guests, as you'd expect in a place like that, were all highly successful. Everything was polished, cultivated, sophisticated; we were all enjoying the fruits of the best that life has to offer. Or so we thought. One day, the immaculate routine of life around the pool was disturbed. There was a flurry of white uniformed hotel staff around one of the sun-worshippers. One of the guests was dying of a heart attack.

And what did the rest of us do? Nothing. We all pretended that nothing was happening. The by now hysterical wife was swept out of the way by some of the staff, and the still dying man was wheeled away on his sun-lounger, so that this intrusion of reality into the super-de-luxe womb of the hotel should not disturb the enjoyment of the other guests. All continued as calmly as before, except that in the mind of every single one of those guests was the knowledge that in a discreet corner of the hotel gardens, a man was acting out his death agony, and his helpless wife was having to stand there and watch him.

As you might imagine, the atmosphere in the hotel was electric, despite all the outward calm. That evening, the restaurant was crowded with people in evening dress, all talking and laughing, and perhaps drinking a little more than usual. Suddenly, the widow appeared at the door. Conversation continued because, after all, we were all far too sophisticated to want to appear interested in her. Like the other women, she was all dressed up and bejewelled. The tension was almost unbearable; was she going to be the ghost at the feast? As she stepped forward into the room, it was seen that she had two companions with her. And all three were talking and laughing as if nothing had happened.

Suddenly, everyone in the place relaxed. It was all right, she wasn't going to make a scene or spoil everyone's holiday by letting any emotion intrude into the place. Admittedly, her careful make-up hadn't quite managed to cover all the signs of pain and terror on her face, but she was OK, she was going to play the white woman, be a good sport. The festivities continued, and Death, who had had the bad taste and bad manners to call unwanted, uninvited and unannounced, was left to make his departure through the servants' exit.

Those of you who have been bereaved may remember that although people were very kind for the first few weeks after the death (that is, the people who would talk to you; you may also have noticed people crossing the street to avoid having to speak to you), after a time even the kindest of friends became impatient with you. "It's time you pulled yourself together; all this sitting around feeling sorry for yourself isn't doing you any good; why don't you get out and make some new friends/put yourself into your work/

join the Bible study group?" (Unspoken message: "You are selfish and self-indulgent. I'm bored with you always looking so sorry for yourself. No one ever feels sorry for me, so why should I waste my time with you?")

If you were lucky enough to have someone who was actually willing to let you be real, who didn't back away if you couldn't keep up a good front, and who gave you space to explore all your highly complex and overwhelming feelings, then the odds are that it was someone (a) who'd been put through the wringer themselves at some time, and (b) who was at peace with themselves – who'd actually been able to befriend all the different parts of their personality.

I spoke before about our preferring animals to humans in a negative sense, in that they are so much easier to control and hold far fewer surprises for us. And perhaps too that with them we are at last able to relax and let the mask drop – that exhausting mask, on which we use up so much of our energy, trying to keep it firmly in place. How desperately sad it is to see that ice-cold man, always so controlled and proper and forbidding, suddenly drop to his knees and fling his arms around his dog, giving it all the warmth and affection he could never give to himself or to another human being. Or that beautifully groomed woman, always first with the name-drop or the bitchy remark, hugging her pet to herself as if trying to squeeze some of the warmth of life into her coldness.

But there is another side to it, that Walt Whitman talks of:

> I think I could turn and live with animals, they are so
>   placid and self-contained,
> I stand and look at them sometimes an hour at a stretch.
> They do not sweat and whine about their condition,
> They do not lie awake in the dark and weep for their
>   sins,
> They do not make me sick discussing their duty to God,

No one is dissatisfied — not one is demented with the
  mania of owning things,
Not one kneels to another, nor to his kind that lived
  thousands of years ago,
Not one is respectable or industrious over the whole
  earth.

I suppose he is talking about animals, but he is also talking about the possibility of a certain kind of person. We'll ignore the placid for the moment, but he also talks about being self-contained, and perhaps the secret is somewhere in there.

Everything we have been talking about in this chapter has been to do with not being self-contained. It has been to do with a basic attitude of mistrust towards oneself; with remaining obedient to those voices programmed into us by parents and society. We have seen how our expectations about life were almost magically moulded by others, while we were still virtually in our cradles. Wherever we go, whatever we do, those tapes can control our journey, affecting the way we see ourselves, other people, reality, and the very meaning and nature of the universe.

What worries me intensely about those of us who say we believe in God, is that we could almost be the models for Whitman's poem. We sweat and whine and lie awake. I am almost daily made sick by the way we discuss and discuss our duty to God. And those who follow other gods fit into this pattern too. People do become demented with the mania of possessions — because, after all, what else does life have to offer them? Or they kneel to others — to Lenin, Luis Palau, John Lennon, the Royal Family, or their own ancestors. Or they bow at the altar of work, achievement and success.

And we all end up like little animals in cages, endlessly going around and around on our treadmills, scrambling like mad, working our little hearts out, and getting precisely . . . nowhere.

And perhaps the answer is that we have *all* followed false gods. We have become like the prophet. Our programming tells us about a certain god, about a certain way of understanding ourselves and reality, and so we go on endlessly running into blank walls, spiritual cul-de-sacs, and missing the truth about almost everything. Because we are prepared to trust or believe what others tell us about ourselves and the meaning of our lives, but the one thing we are not prepared to trust is the evidence of our own eyes and hearts.

Our programming says: "You are basically powerless, and many parts of you are not very nice. Other people, especially important people, will not like you unless you behave. The universe is a dangerous and basically hostile place. You need protection. The only way to get through all this in one piece is to obey all the rules. Stick with the right sort of people. Hold on to what you should believe. Above all, learn to avoid people or experiences which might unsettle your equilibrium, otherwise who knows what may happen? You must believe that life is the way we say it is, because you are not a trustworthy witness. If you don't obey Mummy and Daddy, and you keep insisting on walking on the lines instead of on the squares, then a huge bear will come up from a basement and eat you."

And so on we go, obsessed with our important religious business. And the very person who could save us from this treadmill existence – the donkey, the Child who looks on the world with wondering, trusting eyes – is the one person that we are never going to trust. And life, real life, is the one thing that we are never going to see. In other words, we are so sickeningly religious, so obsessively, idolatrously seeking for God, that we cannot see the angel before our very eyes.

It is Kierkegaard (again!) who sums it all up:

And what does all this mean? It means that everyone for himself, in quiet inwardness before God, shall humble

55

himself before what it means in the strictest sense to be a Christian, admit candidly before God how it stands with him, so that he might yet accept the grace which is offered to everyone who is imperfect, that is, to *everyone* [my italics]. And then no further; then for the rest let him attend to his work, be glad in it, love his wife, be glad in her, bring up his children with joyfulness, love his fellow men, *rejoice in life* [my italics].

And how many Christians does that suggest to you?

Well, a few, praise be! They are the ones who do enjoy life, have a humorous acceptance of their own humanity with all its messiness and imperfection, and the same acceptance of other people's humanity; they love God and their neighbour, and for the rest of it, just get on with the business of living life as lovingly as possible. They see angels all over the place, mostly in other people, and they trust the evidence of their own eyes.

But the rest of us! What joy in life does our religion bring us? Well, there is a sort of phoney joy around in the Church sometimes. It is completely reliant on making sure that you only mix with people who feel and think in exactly the same way that you do. There will be a firm authority structure, to relieve you of the need for personal decision. The rules will be absolutely clear-cut, black and white, so that judgement can be instant, without any problems of ambiguity. And people will make a great song and dance (literally, quite a lot of the time) about how HAPPY they are. I think I can hear the strain of their song now. . . . "I'm H.A.P.P.Y, I'm H.A.P.P.Y., I know I am, I'm sure I am, I'm H.A.P.P.Y."

I suppose it is naughty of me to be cynical. After all, the other great religion to be suffering a massive decline – football – has hymns which are equally as mindless as any of our mutually congratulatory, self-hypnotic little songs of joy. My favourite, for its wonderful use of the English language, is:

'ere we go, 'ere we go, 'ere we go;
'ere we go, 'ere we go, 'ere we go-oh;
'ere we go, 'ere we go, 'ere we go;
'ere we go-oh, 'ere we go.

Now, in case you are curling your lip at that, I suggest a visit to a few Christian establishments where you will hear songs which are even more mind-boggling in their imbecility. At least the football fans are having a good time, and not making any claims to be more worthy than anyone else — except, perhaps, the opposing team. But Christians can sit around saying how wonderfully happy they are, and how much they're looking forward to being saved, when in the next street you've got a ward full of people dying of cancer, filthy "hotels" crammed full of homeless families, and a young prostitute dying from a heroin overdose on a wet doorstep.

H.A.P.P.Y.? Well, yes perhaps, in a mindless sort of way — as long as they manage to avoid noticing the angel confronting them. In other words, as long as they manage to avoid facing up to the reality of who and what they are, and the reality of other people.

The sort of life that Kierkegaard talks about, demands a strong dose of reality. Reality, first, about oneself. Now we've seen just how difficult this can be, but we can make it even more difficult for ourselves by getting carried away with a sort of religious self-flagellation. There is an obscure kind of pride involved in working out just how deeply, deeply sinful we are. But this isn't what we are asked for; we are just asked to be honest — to accept the love of God for all people, and to wait quietly on God, knowing full well who and what we are, and to swallow our pride and accept that love for ourselves as well.

"And then no further", says Kierkegaard. In other words, for heaven's sake stop being professional Christians, and just get on with being professional human beings. Elsewhere, he uses the image of a man rowing a boat. In order to get to where he wants to go, he has to turn his back on his destination, and concentrate on rowing. If you want to put the religious risk in a nutshell, perhaps it is that instead of rowing and concentrating on the reality of the here and now, we are liable to spend our time standing in the middle of the boat, gazing anxiously ahead. No wonder the boat starts rocking, and no wonder we never get anywhere.

So perhaps the time has come to start concentrating on how to row – how to take our lives seriously. We have looked at some of the problems which may prevent us from grasping the reality. Unfortunately, there is one massive problem still in the way. A whale that may swallow us whole, before we have even begun, or an iceberg on which we will be shattered, or a sea fog that will envelop us. To this problem, we sometimes give the name "God".

4

The Dead is Sacred

If you ever get involved in religious broadcasting, public reaction can be a great eye-opener. As long as you stick to the well-trodden paths, all will be well. (That is, 99.5 per cent of the population will ignore you, realizing, probably quite rightly, that you have nothing to say that will be of any help or interest to them, or that will refer in any way to life as they experience it; the other 0.5 per cent can relax as they are taken once again over the old familiar ground.) But if you try, in some pathetic, stumbling way, to say something that will make sense to the average man and woman in the street, the reaction can be electric.

I have learned in a rough school that almost any letter after a broadcast which begins "I greet you in His name . . ." or "I am a regular churchgoer" or "I have been a practising Christian all my life . . .", can be almost guaranteed to contain a stream of carefully aimed and vicious abuse that will knock you sideways.

But it isn't just letters. I have watched behaviour in churches, in theological colleges, and amongst Christians generally, that has been devastating in its viciousness. And I spend a lot of time with its victims: clergy and laity who have been subjected to an intolerable burden of anger, manipulation, hostility, judgement and coldness.

It can be very instructive to spend time in a convent or monastery where clergy go in order to be patched up, before they have to return to the fray in their parishes. Or to spend time talking to people who have been frozen out of congregations, or people who stand on the outside looking in –

eager to pursue their search for meaning, but terrified by what they see when they look at the contents of the churches.

To put it at its most basic: there seems to be an almost unbridgeable gap between what we profess as Christians, and what we actually do. When I wrote a very angry book about the Church, I was almost swamped with letters, calls and visits from hundreds and hundreds of people. Although I virtually had to take out a mortgage with the Post Office to cover the cost of answering letters, it was an incredible privilege to be able to hear from so many.

And the recurring themes, running through all their stories, were these: firstly, that they were deeply committed to finding or following a meaningful, loving way of life; secondly, that they were strongly attracted by the basic message of the Christian Gospel; thirdly, whether inside or outside organized religion, they found the tension between what the Church SAYS and what it actually DOES to be almost intolerable; fourthly, until they read the book, they had always assumed that they were the only person to feel this way.

And the courage of some of these people! The depth of their compassion, the warmth of their humanity — the sheer feeling of reality about them!

In a sense, the experience of sharing with so many "real" people was almost too much for me. To turn from their openness and genuine warmth to the casualty wards of the Church, was like having to return to the trenches after being on leave. So much so, that sometimes when I meet an open, loving, "real" person, who tells me that they are a Christian, I mentally recoil, and can feel myself thinking "I wonder what their problem is?"

Perhaps the world feels the same way. It only takes a few dozen football hooligans to persuade ordinary football lovers that it's wiser to stay away from matches, and watch them safely at home on TV instead. It only takes a few encounters with religious institutions or professional believers, to persuade the ordinary lover of humanity that they'd be safer pursuing their quest somewhere else.

Because when they meet a believer in "God", it is very easy to recognize the messages that come forth. Henry Miller said, "The new always comes in with the sense of violation, of sacrilege. What is dead is sacred; what is new, that is different, is evil, dangerous, or subversive." But what is new is the present – the ever-changing face of reality; and what is different is the "other", anyone or anything outside ourselves, unless we can conveniently arrange to surround ourselves with clones.

In other words, the message to the outsider may be, "You can come in if you will give obedience to the past, and if you are prepared to change into our image. What you are at the moment is not acceptable."

But haven't we heard those sort of voices before? Didn't all the programmes put into us by parents, culture and the Superego play the same sort of tune? "Stick with your own kind. Obey the rules. Life is dangerous. You are not trustworthy. The only way for you to be acceptable or tolerated is to obey . . . believe . . . play the game (our game, with our rules) . . ."

This doesn't just happen in the Church, of course. But in the Church, it can be given a particularly potent thrust, because the whole thing can be neatly encapsulated in the word "God".

Whatever the tape may be that is playing, it can be given awesome power by being made sacred. Suddenly the most outrageous behaviour, the deepest and most unexamined prejudices, are HOLY. This isn't just "Kill a Commie for Christ", or "the Bishop of Rome is the whore of Babylon", but far more subtle and pervasive. Fear and dislike of sexuality; the inability to come to terms with one's personality; resistance to change; the refusal to face up to reality – all these, and many, many more can be made to seem a sacred duty. God becomes nothing more than the obsessive playing and replaying of all the most stultifying and life-denying tapes in our collection.

And the safest place to play those tapes is with a group of like-minded people, who will only ever agree with you, and never, never argue, question or suggest alternative approaches. Such places are often called "churches", and the person in charge of the master-copy of the tapes is often called "the minister".

The reason for all this is not too hard to find. Perhaps we can see a hint of it, by examining one of the most potent of all the myths in the Bible – Adam and Eve.

Now Adam and Eve offer us a vision of paradise; of what it was, in religious terms, to be perfectly happy – to be perfect. So if we take the story at face value, what is this state of perfection from which we have fallen, and to which we long to return? The Garden of Eden is seen as a place where there is never any want or need to work; there is no anxiety or guilt, man and woman "were both naked, and were not ashamed". Perhaps if you can remember a perfect day from when you were a little child, it would have been much the same; no need to do anything except enjoy life, and be looked after.

But there is danger in the garden – a tree, which gives understanding ("the knowledge of good and evil"). A taste of its fruit, and "the eyes of both were opened". Their first experience of knowledge is to undergo anxiety and guilt; they make themselves clothes, and hide from God. And their punishment for gaining knowledge? Woman is to suffer pain in childbirth, and to feel desire for her man, and man is condemned to work for his living. Finally, God drives them out of the garden, in case they should also eat from the tree of eternal life. Knowledge of good and evil, *and* eternal life, would turn them into rival gods.

So what is the "before" and "after" state of Adam and Eve? "Before" feels remarkably like an idealized version of childhood – a sort of beautiful womb, without any need to make decisions or do anything except relax and enjoy the place. And "after"? Well, it's interesting to look at just what are seen as punishments, these terrible torments that characterize what it means to have been expelled from paradise; and they are, quite simply, work and sexual desire.

Now work, as you'll agree from that feeling of depression on Monday mornings, can be a major pain. But it is also the opportunity to create, to take responsibility for one's life, to provide the means of caring for oneself and one's dependants. Adam is condemned to grow his own food and to make his own bread. But making, creating, achieving, are all vital parts of our lives. It is one of the crucial challenges to Western culture to try to find other ways of affirming people's identities, now that the path of finding identity through one's work is becoming limited to the privileged people who can find employment. It would be utterly sick to go to Tyneside or a Welsh mining village, and start talking about "work" as a punishment.

And sexual desire – is that a punishment? Well, there's a very long tradition in the Church that might suggest it is. Religion and sex make very uneasy bedfellows, if you'll pardon the expression. Sex, almost more than any other subject, will set the parental and cultural tapes churning into overdrive. Just close your eyes for a moment, and try to remember the rules, spoken and unspoken, that you were given as a child. Was it Lord Curzon, on his wedding night, who turned away from his bride with enormous distaste and said "Ladies don't move"?

Sex can create anxiety, guilt, conflict. Its power can be disturbing, to say the least. Origen, one of the early Christian fathers, castrated himself in order to escape the problem. And yet it is also one of the most beautiful and precious parts of our humanity, not a punishment, but a GIFT from God.

And yet how intensely annoying it can be for us "good" religious folk, to meet someone who actually enjoys sex, and relishes their humanity. No wonder we have a field-day of self-righteous tongue-clacking when issues like venereal disease or AIDS raise their ugly heads. "God's judgement", we say, with a pleased little smirk. That'll teach those dirty little beggars to have fun, when the only kick we can get out of it is to pore over the Sunday papers, breathing in every last word, and making sure not to miss out on the next edition so that we can find yet more horrendous details to disapprove of.

One of the holiest people I've ever met is a rabbi. He is so deeply down to earth, so truly "Christian" as I'd have to put it, in his acceptance and love of humanity, his warmth, wisdom and understanding, that I, as a "professional" Christian, felt quite taken aback. Little warning tapes started playing in my mind, saying "Oh really, that's not quite nice is it?" He'd been to visit the home of a saint, which is now preserved as a shrine. "Where's the lavatory?", he asked, to be met with terribly shocked looks, and the reproving remark that that unfortunate part of the house had been converted into something else. Saints, of course, cannot go to the lavatory. They can think wonderful thoughts, fly, and appear in two places at once, but we simply couldn't cope with the thought that they might also be normal human beings, with normal human bodies and appetites.

This same rabbi trained in all the approved religious places, and was almost stifled by all the religious attitudes. There were all the trappings of religion, but little sign of God. So he ran away to Amsterdam, and there in the bars, in nights of tenderness and gentleness with strangers, he found God. I hope he won't get me wrong if I say that he is one of the most truly Christian people that I have ever met.

And the same applies to someone I met at a conference for

people dealing with AIDS victims. He is the head consultant at one of Britain's largest clinics for sexually transmitted diseases. Now he really set my tapes whirring into action. Liberal, loving attitudes . . . my eye! I stared at him with the deepest distaste, and may even have edged slightly away from him, when he told me that until the arrival of AIDS, the special clinic had always been the happiest place to work in hospital.

Perhaps he noticed the twitch on my face, as I fought to keep down a sneer of embarrassment. Anyway, he explained with great kindness that in his opinion it was only nice people who contracted VD. It was the people outside who tended to be cold, judgemental, unfeeling and unconcerned. AIDS had brought tragedy into a department, which until then had been full of warmth and affection and the sound of laughter.

As you read that, perhaps you can feel or hear the tapes roaring into action. For myself, they play so loudly that it has taken an awfully long time for me to try to understand what he was saying; an awfully long time to work out how I actually feel about what he told me, rather than what my tapes tell me I should feel.

And that's the problem about sex – it can be so difficult for us to deal with. The simplest way out is to accept that it IS a punishment; life would be a lot simpler if we could be without it. And perhaps that's the key to the thought of work and sex being punishments – we want life to be simple. Simple as it was when the grown-ups made all the decisions and did all the work. Simple as it was when we were, in a sense, parasites, reliant on them for food, warmth, shelter, approval, everything.

In other words, perhaps the message of the Garden of Eden is that deep down, what we really want is for someone to look after us; to take the problems, ambiguities and anxieties away from us, and tuck us up in a nice warm cosy bed with a nightlight and a hot drink.

If you are married, or part of a committed relationship, have you ever felt an intense anger towards your partner when they failed to act in such a cosseting, parental way towards you? We all do, at some stage or other, and that's fine if both partners know what they're doing; but when the need or demand is hidden, then disaster can strike. It'd be hopeless to generalize from divorce statistics, but a recurring theme, which comes up time and time again when you're dealing with marriages that are breaking up, is that there has been an unacknowledged demand from either or both partners, that they should be looked after. In other words, that wife should really be mother (or be as much as possible like the husband's real mother), or husband should be father (or as much as possible like the wife's real father).

Some analysts would even go so far as to say that we all marry people who in some way relate to our image of father or mother. The crunch comes when we have to see whether we can cope with the reality of the very different individual to whom we are married. It can be amazingly stressful to have to come to terms with the uniqueness and complete difference of another human being – to move from fantasy to reality.

It's all a risk; relationship is a risk; exploring the language of sex with your partner is a risk . . . but a punishment, surely not? In fact these two punishments of work and sex are in reality gifts – part of the glory of what it is to be human, and to venture along the paths of self-understanding, creativity, and exploring the mystery of another's being.

But there is the model for us, in the story of the Garden. The best state of all is to be back in the womb; the glory of being human, rather than a divine pet, is a punishment; we belong, so they tell us, to a "fallen world". Perhaps some of us would want to say that if what it means to be fallen is to take an adult responsibility for one's life then, with the German philosopher Hegel, we'd have to say that it was a "fall upwards".

But if we hold to the Fall model, then a certain picture of God fits in quite neatly too. God is someone who does not want His creation to have knowledge or understanding; that capacity for moral choice, for making decisions, must be His alone. What is required of humanity is not thought, but obedience.

If this longing to be looked after is a part of all of us, then it is not surprising that, in an age of deep stress and uncertainty, any church which guarantees to pop you back to the Garden of Eden will play to packed houses. In return for obedience and an unquestioning conformity to the rules, you will be given an enormously secure package to see you through life. No wonder fundamentalist religion is seeing such a massive surge in almost every country of the world. And no wonder that those who believe in the beauty of the human spirit are dismayed.

Lionel Trilling, that great champion of the human cause, puts it like this:

> Life presses us so hard, time is so short, the suffering of the world is so huge, simple, unendurable – anything that complicates our moral fervour in dealing with reality as we immediately see it and wish to drive headlong upon it must be regarded with some impatience.
>
> (*The Liberal Imagination*)

And that's precisely the point. This Adam and Eve God is like a huge buffer that we put between ourselves and reality. It is a way of imposing order on all the disorder and ambiguity of our existence. It is a way of refusing to face up to the task of being an adult human being. All that is required is to obey.

At the very least, this is an immoral attitude. Ethical choice, the search for the true and the good, becomes nothing more than a question of obedience. No wonder groups of Christians in Nazi Germany could spend the war discussing prayer book revision, or that the entire bench of bishops in the House of Lords could vote in favour of slavery. (This isn't strictly relevant, but did you know that the hymn, "How sweet the name of Jesus sounds", was written by the captain of a slave ship as he crossed the Atlantic with his latest cargo of human death and misery?) Conform, stick with the group, obey the tapes, never take the risk of confronting reality – and give all this the name of God.

No wonder there was a group of theologians who spoke happily about the "death of God". What they were saying, in part, was that mankind could never undertake a truly religious quest until they had got rid of the smothering God; the God who is nothing more than an insurance against anxiety, and an obedience to the parental voices that can control and master our lives. "When a man prays," wrote Ugo Betti, "do you know what he's doing? – He's saying to himself: 'Keep calm, everything's all right; it's all right'."

To go right back to the beginning, this is the voice of the prophet. And if we follow the prophet, then it may well be that the God we worship is nothing more than a sacralization of all the programming we dare not disconnect.

The motto of my theological college was "Guard the Deposit". It is a quote from one of the very last of the Epistles, when the Church had lost its initial drive and fervour, and was left with the task of consolidating and maintaining its legacy from the past. The Victorian founders of the college had emblazoned this motto everywhere, including, somewhat unfortunately, on the inside of the elaborate chamber pots.

The Church ruled by the prophet will see its task in just such a way. "Guard the Deposit." Hold on to the known. And, of course, amongst the "known" must be God Himself. That is why the ancient formulae must be protected so fervently. Better the dead butterfly you've got pinned down, than a field full of new species you can't quite get hold of. And if your basic feeling about yourself is that you are not very nice, then it is far better to have a totem who will remind you of this, than to risk being confronted by a living God who might actually make you feel good about yourself.

The prophet's God is big on punishment. (Remember that ambivalent feeling about authority? You need ruthless strength to keep things in control, but your love for it is a strange mixture of fear and duty.) Guilt is one of his mightiest weapons. The love he gives is ambiguous, to say the least. You will be loved and accepted, IF . . .

There is something deeply tragic about this kind of love we crave. It goes right back to the cradle, and to that feeling of absolute dependence on the omnipotent adults who alone could feed us and protect us. And as we grew more conscious, so we learned how to behave if they were to love us. A smile here, a rule to be obeyed there. We will love you, if . . . The child searches its parents' faces to see how it is doing; do they approve, do they disapprove?

One of the most terrible cases I have ever come across, was that of a little four-year-old girl. Over a period of twenty-four hours, her father punished and beat her because he felt she was not minding him. With the mother's help, the child was beaten to death with belts and whips. After about twenty hours of this torture, the dying little girl dragged herself to her father, because she needed his help to go to the lavatory. He was systematically murdering her, and yet she needed him because he was her father and she wasn't old enough to undo the clasps on her trousers. Amidst all the torture and brutality, she had been too well-behaved a little girl to wet herself.

Once upon a time, you and I were that helpless, and we too learned what we must do in order to be loved. That feeling of helplessness will always be with us, together with that need to win approval. But we have the choice of letting it rule us, or else of accepting that it is a part of us, hearing its voice and treating it with compassion, but choosing to find our own way. When we worship the prophet's God, we are letting our lives be controlled by the hurt little child in us. It is the giant, magical images from our past that are controlling our present. The reality of who we are NOW, and the reality of the life around us, is unseen and unheard.

Even that great theologian Paul Tillich was not immune to the magic. He said that the greatest and most difficult task of every Christian was to "accept that you are accepted". There is truth there, of course, but danger too. Somewhere deep inside we feel unacceptable. Everyone else is normal. No one else hurts. (Or else, perhaps, the perverted and dangerous inversion of that feeling; I am normal. I am all right. Everyone else is sick/wrong/unlovable/unacceptable.) And so we long for that most powerful figure of all to tell us that we are loved, really, despite everything.

But the figure is still something outside ourselves. It may be real, or it may just be our programming again. And will we ever believe something that comes from outside ourselves? Won't it just be another parental pat on the head? We can spend our entire lives accumulating those little pats. We can win Nobel prizes; become international celebrities, adored by millions; we can sleep with a thousand different "lovers"; do everything just right, pass every single test that we feel life is setting us . . . and yet, deep down inside, do we really feel any better?

This feeling of loss and incompleteness can be so strong that the only answer can seem to long for the afterlife. In heaven, everything will be made all right. Everything in the present can safely be counted as loss, as long as we know that there will be another chance, another bite at the cherry; somehow it will all come right in the end. And so we long for immortality, when we don't even know what to do with ourselves on a wet Sunday afternoon. We long to win approval and the final prize from God. You might say that our longing for heaven is in almost direct proportion to our inability to make anything meaningful of our life NOW. And always, always, we feel that the love and approval have got to come from outside. Not for a moment do we dare to consider that the one sort of love and approval we need to win is *our own*.

If you want to put that in theological language, perhaps you could say that there is a conflict of gods. There is the outside authority; the all-seeing eye that watches and judges us, and may occasionally intervene. But there is another way of talking about God, also familiar in the Christian tradition. This tends to say puzzling and difficult things like "God is within you"; so puzzling, and so difficult in fact, that although we may pay lip-service to such an idea, we dare not explore its implications.

In the bad old days, when Ireland was virtually split up into huge estates, there was a very distinct hierarchy. At the top, usually unseen and unknown, were the landlords. The income from the land would be channelled to them, often in England, where they could lead lives of wealth and sophistication. If they were absentee landlords, then there would be a hierarchy of stewards, agents and overseers, to make sure that the estate ran smoothly, and provided them with enough money. At the bottom of the pack, after the tenant farmers, came the peasants and labourers; people who could only speculate, if they had the energy left, about the nature of the person for whom they slaved. They could only guess at such a person through what they saw of his minions.

If you applied such a model to talk about the conflicting gods, then the absentee landlord would be one way of looking at God. There is power of life or death, and absolute obedience is required for the orders that are filtered down through the hierarchy. Everything "good" that comes from humanity is really his; in comparison to the splendour of his life, the daily grind of the peasants seems unimportant, and rather unpleasant. You can't compare a mansion in Belgravia with a dirty hovel, reeking of peat smoke. The most important person is at the top of the scale; the least important is at the bottom. But another way of looking at it would be to say that the person at the top of the scale is the least important. Their existence, somewhere over the water, living the sort of life which it would be impossible to imagine, speaking a different language and holding different beliefs and values, is of negligible importance. What is important is the life of the people who are actually there; their sickness and poverty; their births and deaths, and loves and hopes; their despair and tiredness; their dreams and fantasies; their sweat and failure and success . . . every jot and iota that goes to make up their life. There, at the very heart of their existence, is God.

But in order to find God there, it is necessary to jettison the other God. The one excludes the other, or, as the mediaeval mystic Meister Eckhart put it, we need to risk "man's last and highest parting, when for God's sake he takes leave of God". To bring the wheel full circle, we need to tell the prophet to shut up, and start listening to what the donkey has to tell us.

And this will mean getting rid of certainty. If we get rid of the absentee landlord, the structures may start crumbling. However abject our poverty and slavery, we may well prefer the comfort of staying in a clearly defined role. However brutal and uncaring the landlord, at least he has the ultimate responsibility for our lives. But this demand for certainty can be stultifying; it can freeze us in our tracks, and rob us of any hope of growth or change. To all those fundamental questions at the beginning of the book, he may be able to give us an answer – but whether we can actually believe him, without anaesthetizing huge portions of our understanding and experience, is another question. Life is so complex and ambiguous, that it may be that the only things about which we can be absolutely certain are dead things; the dead cannot move or change. We can be fairly certain of a brick or a tomb. Perhaps we can be fairly certain of a dead god.

5

What's in a Name?

But supposing we take the risk of attempting to take a donkey's-eye-view of theology — that is, of questions of ultimate importance — what might we see? Well, there's a problem here, because, as we pointed out in the beginning, the experts have all the words. But at the moment, we are ignoring what the prophet has to say, with all his extensive and expert vocabulary, because of the fear that his conditioning, including his image of God, are the very things that prevent him from seeing reality. So we will have to treat words with care, especially abstract formulae, because that is not how the donkey expresses herself. She runs away, grinds to a halt, and lies down. When she speaks to the prophet, it is to remind him of their history together. The one word she does not (cannot?) use, is "God".

And perhaps that is the road we have to follow, if we are to avoid running away from the questions, or if we are to avoid ignoring the reality of God by concentrating on the theories about God. But can you have a book about religion which can ignore the word "God"? The job of this chapter is to try to explain what I'll be trying to say when I use that difficult word.

Those of you who have read Kenneth Grahame's magical book, *The Wind in the Willows*, will remember the chapter called "The Piper at the Gates of Dawn". In what must be one of the most beautiful passages in all children's literature, Grahame describes the search of Mole and Ratty for a baby otter who has been lost. A poor swimmer, the otter has been missing for days, and there is fear that he may have been drowned at the weir. Mole and Ratty search all night, and then with the dawn a strange music leads them to a secret island. With a growing sense of awe and wonder, they come ashore and make their way to a clearing. And there, for one breathless moment, against the clearness of the dawning sky, they see the god Pan standing watch over the sleeping baby otter. They fall down in worship. The rising sun dazzles them, and when at last they can see again, the vision has vanished. Only little Portly is left safely behind.

People who want to use God-talk could approach this story in several different ways. For a start, the atheist might say: "The animals had an experience of awe and wonder. The fact that people have religious 'experiences' (whatever that may mean) is not evidence for the fact that there is someone or something that they have experienced. The only thing that you can say is that they had a feeling." The atheist might go on to prove, in a thoroughly respectable manner, that the very idea of the god Pan is nonsense.

Then the theist might butt in, "Ah, but the fact that the animals had that experience proves that there is a god Pan. We know that Pan exists, and that he is infinitely powerful, wise and good; he is both the maker and the preserver of the whole animal universe. Who created the animals if he did not? He is all-loving, and wishes his creation nothing but good. The fact that the otter was found safely proves all this."

Getting a little heated, the atheist then points out that 48.3 otters are drowned at the weir annually, and how does this fit in with a loving Pan? The theist may reply with stories of miraculous rescues from the foam, or may say that since the weir was man-made, how can Pan be blamed for casualties. Back comes the statistic that 7.6 otters die from disease or natural disaster; a) why does Pan allow that? and b) why aren't they miraculously saved too? Hopefully, the theist doesn't then try to prove that they were very sinful otters, but he may say that although he accepts the figures, they make no difference to the fact that he knows that Pan is a loving god. "Anyway," he says, "just look at those hoof-prints in the ground. They are proof that Pan was there." "Nonsense," replies the other, "those are natural marks in the soil. They tell us nothing."

Eventually, the atheist and the theist set up a very bad-tempered camp on the island, and stand watch over the clearing. "This is Pan's garden, which he tends, and that's why there's a clearing, and why he has left his hoof-prints." "Those are not hoof-prints, nor is this a garden. If I am to believe you, you must show me some concrete evidence. We'll see if your god Pan comes along . . ."

After a fortnight, all that has happened is that they have both got very wet and even more bad tempered. One still says that there is no evidence to believe in Pan. Indeed, there appears to be no visible difference between Pan being there, or Pan not being there. What, if anything, are they talking about, except a product of the theist's imagination? The other agrees that they have not seen Pan, but still insists that he exists and that he believes in him. And perhaps we had better leave them there; they can go home and fight it out, as they have been doing for centuries. After all, they are neither of them going to make any important difference to anyone's life.

But while those two old bores have been battling it out, other voices have been waiting patiently. There is a very fashionable voice which says something like, "The point at issue is not whether the god Pan exists or not. You can only make meaningful remarks about things which can be proved or disproved. When I say 'this is a chair', I can prove that to you, and so the remark makes sense. If I say 'the god Pan exists' there is no way in which we can show that the remark is true or false. So it is better not to make the remark at all. When I say that I believe in the god Pan, what I really mean is that all the stories about Pan provide me with a guide as to how I ought to behave. Pan provides me with a vision of life, and a code of behaviour for what I believe to be the most meaningful life possible. By following him, I hope to become more Pan-like. The only sense in which you can 'test' my story about Pan, is to live it. It is an invitation to a way of life, not a set of theories about someone or something who may or may not exist."

Last of all to speak, and timidly at that, is the donkey-voice. We feel timid to speak, because what everyone else has said seems so logical; what we want to say is more difficult, and we are straining to find words that won't sound silly. But we feel forced to speak, because nothing that has been said so far is quite adequate for the complexity of what we sense has happened.

"Pan was there", "Pan was not there", say the theist and the atheist. "If you felt awestruck, it must have been by something (or nothing) that can be proved (or disproved)." But words have run out for the donkey-voice; who can honestly say what happened? Perhaps the easy way out is to join forces with the third voice; after all, how you live your life, stripped of childish hopes of reward or punishment, is the central issue. And yet, is that all we want to say?

When the donkey was remonstrating with the prophet, she reminded him of their story together. And perhaps here the donkey-voice would want to remind us of all that has gone to make up the story. The desperate search for the lost; the agony of the parents, and the distress of Mole and Ratty. The fear of drowning and of animal traps; the strange journey through the darkness; the calling music (pan-pipes? the wind in the reeds?); the sense of joy and of coming home; finally, the joy of seeing the little otter safely asleep at the feet of . . . of what? Grahame gives us no name for the presence. The sense of worship and of love, and then the fading of the vision; the slow return home as the memory fades, until they are unable to remember anything specific. Was it a vision or a dream? Were they dazzled by the sun, and the uprush of emotion.

"I feel as if I had been through something very exciting and rather terrible, and it was just over, and yet nothing particular had happened", says the Mole. A sound like far-away music accompanies them . . . the wind in the reeds? "Music . . . but with words in it, too – it passes into words and then out of them again . . ." . . . "But what do the words mean?", asked the wondering Mole. "That I do not know", said the Rat simply.

For the donkey-voice, to talk about "God" is not the same as talking about half a pound of fish-fingers. It is pushing language to the very limits of what we can say without falling into gibberish. Indeed, it risks falling into nonsense, but what else can you do if you want to give word to what matters to you most? "The lost was found! The pain and suffering of the parents and searchers was important, more than important. The life of the baby otter was important, more than important. Indeed, the whole venture, past, present and future, the beauty of the moment, the centrality of the characters and their emotions, was something so important, something about which I care so much, that I can hardly find words for it. But if you force me, then all I can say is that Pan was there, because that is the only way that I can find to say that this whole event was something of lasting significance, going to the very depths of what is of value to me. And even when I have said that, I still feel that something is missing. '. . . it passes into words and then out of them again . . .'."

Fortunately, we are not alone in wanting to push language to its limits. We have the company of lovers, clowns and poets. It was T. S. Eliot who called poetry "a raid on the inarticulate":

> . . . Words strain,
> Crack and sometimes break, under the burden,
> Under the tension, slip, slide, perish,
> Decay with imprecision, will not stay in place,
> Will not stay still. . .

W. H. Auden left notes about a poem that he was unable to write, in which he was going to express exactly what he meant when he said "I love you". But language failed him, because "I cannot know exactly what I mean". Earlier, we asked how it would be possible to sum up the person one loves in a simple form of words, and decided that language would fail us. But that doesn't mean that we wouldn't want to try. But here again, we'd be pushing at the outer limits of language, far from the secure centre where a chair is a chair, a fish is a fish, and Christmas Day falls on 25th December.

Moving along the outer limits, we would almost certainly bump into the clowns, because they too want to say that life is stranger and more complex than the bureaucrats would have us believe. A comic like Ken Dodd will take you on a magical mystery tour into a strange land where the normal rules of logic are suspended, and language is contorted and extended. As he says, "The word is a container of meaning and if you can open the box, take the meaning out and put another meaning in, it is quite a clever little trick." "What a beautiful day, Missus. What a beautiful day for rushing into the maternity ward and shouting 'It's your fault for voting Labour'."

Like the lovers, the clowns and the poets, Christians long to say all that we can, and more, about ourselves and others involved in the human venture, as people with a past and a future. What happens matters. People matter. And in order to do this, we have to leave the neatly ordered world of strictly rational language. We want to say more than is allowed in the tidy world of mainstream language. In the horror film we spoke about in the Trailer, the crew are confronted by a very real problem; there is a monster on board; their lives are at risk; they are terrified. But the computer is unable to help them, because its language is too logical to understand such things. All it can say, in answer to their frantic questions, is "Does not compute". Some help! And strictly logical language gives us the same sort of answer, if we try to talk about the things that are most meaningful in our lives.

Perhaps one of the reasons why we felt so unhappy about what the atheist and the theist had to say, was that they were using the word "God" as easily as they might use the word "foot". Just because there is a label, they are making the assumption that there must be some "thing" for the label to be describing. But words aren't that easy. I can talk glibly about the Renaissance, but that doesn't necessarily mean that there was such a thing as "Renaissance", that I can prove or disprove. In fact, I'm using the word as a handy tag to talk about a certain movement in history; it is a helpful way of looking at the past.

In the same way, words like "love", "pride", "hate", "joy", have no reality in themselves. When we use them, we are talking about a process that is going on in a human being. But our very use of the words can obscure the reality for us; by using them as labels, they become "things" that we want to have or to get rid of. In the same way, we tend to talk of faith as being a thing that we want to acquire, or that we envy others for having. "I really envy you your (possession of) faith", said a young man. But, again, it is not a "thing" that you can have, but it is a process, an inner activity of which you are the subject. It was as if we were talking about two totally different subjects. He was using the word "faith" as though it were something as easily handled and controlled as a jar of marmalade . . . "You have got a 'faith'; I want to have a 'faith'; give me a 'faith'."

But there is no such thing as a "faith". The word is a useful way of trying to talk about a whole history that I am involved in. How could I give the young man my sleepless nights, moments of despair, comedy or hope at hospital bedsides, a lifelong search for meaning, the fearful sense of deep love? And those are only scratching the surface of the process, which you might describe with the word faith, in which I am engaged.

I went to the hospital to have an X-ray done. After I'd waited for some time, a nurse came to call me. "Is Richard there?" I expect it was said in the best interests of friendliness and good public relations, but I felt very angry. I was a stranger amongst strangers. The nurse did not know me, and would probably never see me again. All I wanted was for someone to X-ray my leg. As far as the hospital was concerned, I was Mr MacKenna, possible fracture. What right did the nurse have to use my Christian name? It was as if she was laying claim to know me, all the different thoughts and feelings and experiences that make up my life. Mr MacKenna is a stranger in a public place, probably with a public persona. Richard is someone much more complex. I expect she wanted to make it seem more personal, but just because of that I felt uneasy. What did she really know of me? In a sense, Mr MacKenna is a useful label; he is the patient with a damaged leg. But "Richard" is not a label. It describes all that goes to make up my life. For someone to use it properly, without devaluing it, they would need to know me very well, and to have shared some of the experiences that are part of the reality of my existence.

And God? Well, God is not a thing either. You can't summon God from the back of the queue, or sum up God, just by bandying the name around. We feel uneasy with a lot of religious talk because it sounds so presumptuous. Most of us believe that our convictions and attitudes about life can only be held with the degree of firmness that experience and evidence allow. If you tell me that hungry lions are always warm and friendly, I may choose to believe you; my attitude may change, though, after a few sleepless nights in the jungle. People who use religious language in much the same casual way that they might compose a shopping list, sound enviably confident. They sound as if they "have" God, and "have" faith, but can we join them, without closing down large areas of our own experience and knowledge? In the past, you could claim that religion had the answer to everything, but now we see that there are so many different ways of understanding the world – personal, political, economic, scientific, sociological, religious ... you pays your money, and you takes your choice. None of them necessarily excludes the others; it is just that we no longer believe that there is one supreme vantage point from which the whole of our experience of life can be understood, any more than the nurse could understand me simply by using my first name.

We live in a world which is constantly changing. Our understanding of our own nature is that we have to change, to grow, to develop, in order to survive as individuals. If institutions are unable to adapt to changing circumstances, they die or atrophy. That seems healthy. Of course, we long for stability and permanence, but how does our Western religious tradition of the best things being unchanging and unchangeable, fit into the reality of life as we experience it?

We also live in a world that is multi-faith, multi-cultural. Does my God mean that the Hindu/Muslim/Buddhist/ Jewish God is wrong? From what standpoint is it possible to assess who is right or who is wrong?

If you take these features of our life seriously, it is hard to understand how one can use God-talk in a matter of fact way. Straightforward out and out theism raises more questions than it answers. What difference does the existence of this all-powerful, all-loving God make in the world? The answers such belief gives us seem too simplistic for the complexity of the questions that life poses us. More, there is a risk of passing the cosmic buck. If mankind is slowly and painfully learning one thing, it is that we are responsible for our own lives, and for the life of this whole planet. We have to decide whether we want to blow ourselves to smithereens, to pollute the environment, destroy whole life-forms, over-populate until we are unable to feed ourselves . . . no outside force will come and decide this for us. The responsibility for the future is ours, and ours alone.

Slowly and painfully, then, we try to find the words for a donkey-theology. All the arguments of those who want to prove or disprove the existence of God, or the validity of religion, leave us cold. It's all far more complex than their words will allow. But neither are we happy just to say that our belief is a way of talking about taking a certain moral position in life. We want to say more than that. We want to push language to its limits in order to talk about the human concern. But then, how can we express ourselves?

The answer goes back to the donkey, who reminded the prophet of their story together; back, too, to the donkey-voice who wanted to talk about all that had happened to Mole and Ratty. We tend to think of our religious tradition in terms of long sets of logical propositions which have been handed down to us. But the most valuable resource we have contains nothing of that. "God", for the Christian, is a word given to us in the context of many different collections of stories, myths, legends, songs, narratives, and moral codes – the Bible. If the nurse had wanted to understand something about "Richard", then she would have to have shared something of my story. If we want to understand something of the complexity and ambiguity of our existence – a venture that will take us far from the heartlands of neatly ordered logical propositions – then we need something as complex and ambiguous as stories to help us.

You can see this struggle going on in the Bible, with the prophet voice demanding clarity and certainty, and the donkey-voice struggling to hang on to the richness and complexity of the story. Moses is called to free his people from slavery in Egypt, but who calls him? The voice defines itself in a personal and particular way: "I am the God of your father, the God of Abraham, the God of Isaac, and the God of Jacob." In other words, in order to understand who or what you are dealing with, you will need to look pretty closely at the stories of these particular individuals. But Moses foresees problems: the Israelites will want to know something much more concrete about whoever or whatever they are dealing with – they will want to know a name, to have a label; it simply won't be enough to ask them to reflect on the stories of their ancestors. "If they ask me 'what is his name?' what shall I say to them?" The voice replies, "I am who I am". This could possibly be the single most unhelpful remark in the Bible. What on earth does it mean?

If you look at a hundred different commentaries on the book Exodus, you will find about a hundred different answers. But at the core of them all is the fact that this is a refusal to give a neat label or definition. Moses is not told, "I am the unmoved mover, omnipotent, omnipresent, omnicompetent; you'll find my c.v. in forty-eight volumes of St Thomas Aquinas." Instead, the answer is more like, "That's for me to know, and you to find out", or even, "I am me". In effect, Moses is told to go to the Israelites and say, "Someone called Me has sent me to you". This will not be made any easier by the fact that Moses is a murderer, just returned from a long exile in a foreign land, and with a speech impediment.

Life does not get any simpler for Moses. "Me" is still remarkably hard to tie down, and can only be wondered at through a series of strange events – a fire or a cloud, towards which you march through unfamiliar, frightening ground, but which you never seem to reach. Who, or what, is involved in this whole venture? Many of the Israelites have no doubt – the whole business is Moses' doing from beginning to end. "This is all your fault. At least we were comfortable as slaves. Why did you bring us out to die in the desert?"

Matters come to a head at Sinai. While Moses is on the mountain, the people try to understand just what exactly has happened to them. On the one hand, they have the difficult donkey-voice which says that they have been dealing with "Me" – someone who will only hint at what they might be, by asking you to look at what happened to individuals in past events, and to explore what is happening to you now. But how can you get a grip on someone called "I am who I am" or "I will be what I will be"? This is all just too difficult and ambiguous for the prophet voice, which prefers either to put the whole thing down to Moses, or else to try to win back religious control of the situation. The answer is to make the golden calf. Now this is the ideal god for the prophet. You can see it, touch it, give it a name, and carry it around with you. Being gold, it probably reflects back your own image. And, of course, it provides a very clear and unambiguous answer. "You want to know who to thank for your freedom? You want a direct, uncomplicated package that will sort out all these bothersome questions? Well, here it is; this is the god who brought you safely out of Egypt."

And this argument was to be the central issue of Israel's history. The deliverance from Egypt was the key to their understanding of themselves as a people. But how to understand the deliverance? Egyptian foreign policy? A great human leader? Or this maddening "other", which steadfastly refuses to explain itself except by pointing you back to the actual event – "I am the I am who brought you out of the land of Egypt . . ."? Those who seek clear definitions, and to be in complete control of the situation, will find other golden calves; Israel needs a king, an army, a bureaucracy, to take part in international politics . . . being Israel is about being in control, it is about strength and power politics. The other voice is harder to hear; being Israel means to stand humbly and in awe before the story of mercy and justice which brought us into being as a people; unless there is a deep trust in the undefinable one who delivered us, then we will just become a nation like any other nation.

The risk is there for the Christian too. We are given a collection of stories to deal with. But stories are puzzling and difficult; who or what, exactly, are we trying to deal with? We may prefer to make a golden calf, painfully distilling the "truth" (as we see it) from the unrefined material. But the danger is the same. We end up with a man-made god, neatly locked up in man-made words. But what relation does this easily identified "thing" have to do with what really matters – our daily life, our history, and the way we are involved socially, politically and economically with our fellows and the world around us?

To put it another way, the central issue for all of us is that of human history: how we tell it, how we live it, whether it has a future. All of us, like it or not, are involved in the living and making of the human story, and the story of our own particular lives. There is the great question of whether or not the human story will be able to continue, and if it does continue, whether it will be more or less human. There is the particular question of whether we can find any pattern or meaning in our lives; whether we can actually live out the story of our lives, or whether we will be swept along like passive spectators, and suddenly realize as we lie dying, that the whole thing has been about as interesting and meaningful for us as a half-watched episode of "Cross-roads".

"God is within you", we said earlier. But to find that "within" means learning how to listen to our own story. We saw, just from the little snippet of Mole and Ratty, how involved a story can be. You can only wrench clear-cut answers from it if you maul it around, and ignore all the parts you don't want to see. And then the answers are the wrong ones. The prophet probably had all the logical answers about God, but he was so oblivious to the reality of his own story, that he missed out on the real thing. To hear our own story, we need to lose that element of control – of forcing it in the direction we think it ought to be going.

It is somewhere deep in the mystery of who we *really* are, that the answers will be found. And the more we dare to explore that reality, the more we will find that there is something – I cannot give it a name – that links all humanity. In some strange way, the more we discover our own uniqueness, the closer we come to others in their uniqueness. And at the heart of it all . . . ah, then perhaps we may dare to start using that risky language about God.

6

One Man's Story

Perhaps, like me, you sometimes feel that you would like to give the Old Testament a wide berth. All this talk of Moses and I Am is too confusing. At least things are more straightforward in the New Testament. After all, don't we know that Jesus is true God and true man? Why all this fuss about a simple word like God?

And yet, if we approach the gospels from a donkey's eye level, trying to see them at face value, without reading into them all the things that the prophet tells us ought to be there, then a strange new world awaits us. In a sense, the argument continues from the Old Testament; the battle is between those who want to be in control of the situation – we find them building golden calves all over the place, and even struggling to turn Jesus into one, if they can get their hands on him – and those who are prepared to be with Jesus, without trying to take him over.

In this chapter, I am going to try to look at a very little of the story which Mark's gospel gives us. In a sense, it will be a dry run for looking at our own stories, because many of the old familiar voices are at work here too. It may seem risky to tread where so many experts have been before. "The theology of Mark's gospel is X or Y", they tell us, and we nod in timid agreement – after all, they are the experts. But whoever wrote this story has been dead for nearly two thousand years, and came from a background that we can only guess at. All we have is the story he left us, and ourselves. To bear fruit, we need to make friends of the story, and to let it play around in our minds. All that matters is what it says to us. We will need to be equally firm when we come to tell our own stories; otherwise we will find some expert stepping in and telling us what they think we ought to know. We need courage just to be donkeys, and to be honest about what we feel confronts us. But let's just listen to a few of the voices that are around in the gospel.

The first set of voices are the religious establishment. Although they are called scribes, Pharisees, priests and doctors of the law, I'd prefer just to call them the professional religious. With our hideous tradition of anti-semitism, it is all too easy to see them as a Jewish problem – the nasties who got rid of Jesus, and whose race has been paying for it ever since. But their attitude is timeless, to be found in every religion. Unfortunately, it has the habit of perpetuating itself through the religious officer-class. Listen to a few speeches from those in control, and you may well believe that Pharisaism is alive and well and living under a different name.

For them, religion is a way of imposing order on experience, and being in control of it. Even God has to work in the approved manner. Like the prophet, their problem is not that they are bad, but that they cannot see what is before their eyes, because it will not fit into the pattern. What authority does Jesus have to act in this way? Why won't He give them a sign from heaven, so that they can know for certain? Because they are convinced that God only works within carefully defined guidelines, and because Jesus does not fit into them, by definition He cannot be on the side of God.

Jesus heals a paralytic, and tells him that his sins are forgiven. He heals on the Sabbath. None of this can be from God, because it does not fit in with the rules. The religious are unable to take seriously the reality of what is happening, because it is out of their control. None of their programming is adequate to help them – and it is too risky for them to trust their own eyes.

Perhaps the last straw for them, is the sort of people that

Jesus attracts. He seems positively to enjoy going around with the wrong crowd. When pressed about this, he comes out with the extraordinary claim "I did not come to invite virtuous people, but sinners". This is a threat to the whole "religious" approach to God.

The particular golden calf here, is the idea that man has somehow to win God's approval before he can be loved or accepted. To win that approval, and to keep in check the chaos monster that he fears lurks within him, the Pharisee sees God in terms of legislation. Responsibility means obedience; sin means disobedience. There is also a subtle form of narcissism, to do with perfecting oneself. What can Jesus possibly mean, to say that the Sabbath was made for man's benefit, rather than that the Sabbath is an un-breakable rule to which man must conform? And how can the son of man (a sort of polite equivalent to saying "one" instead of "I") forgive sins? Only God can forgive. And in order to stay forgivable, you have got to stay within the religious world. People outside are bad; they will con-taminate you. You must stick with your group of like-minded people, all set on self-improvement, and winning approval from God.

And then along comes Jesus, with the horrendous idea that the only people who will not be invited to share God's generosity, are the very ones who have been working so desperately hard to earn it. In other words, that the real religious venture is out of your control. You cannot buy love, or win it. The only thing you have to do is to learn to be yourself; i.e., a sinner.

No wonder such an element of hatred creeps in. Jesus suggests that God is offering for free the very thing that people are trying to buy at such cost. But, of course, if this love is free, it puts the professional religious at a grave disadvantage. They no longer have power or control over people. They can no longer dole out God's love or forgiveness as if it were a commodity. Perhaps all their neat formulae haven't managed to pin down the reality of the living God. What good are books of rules and definitions, when you cannot be sure what it is you are dealing with? At the end of the gospel, they are still as lost as when they started. "We need proof; give us a sign; come down from the cross if you are who you say you are." You can hear the same note of bitterness today, if you suggest that there is no reason at all why everyone should not go to heaven, rather than just Christians. "Then why am I wasting my time being good?" Worse, I suspect that there is a vicious streak in some religion, which takes positive delight in the thought that one day I will get some sort of reward for all this dutiful slog, whereas *they* will be punished for having such a good time. And now is Jesus suggesting that God is on the side of the good-timers, and won't have any room for the religious? Horror!

The battle still goes on. If you produce a book called *Guard the Deposit*, or can inject your religion with absolute certainty, then you can be almost guaranteed record sales or a packed church. We crave certainty – it is a drug; but it is the religion of the golden calf, not of Moses; of the Pharisees, not of Jesus. To have religious certainty, you must lead a religious life; encounter with God comes through withdrawing from a "profane" world into a "sacred" world. When you build the golden calf, you can say very exactly what you are doing; if you follow Moses it is all much more complex – somewhere in this story of our struggle for freedom and justice, and the long painful slog through the desert, God is to be found. Similarly for Jesus, religion is not something set apart from life, but comes from a deep involvement with those whose feet are firmly planted in reality.

This encounter with reality comes across particularly strongly when you look at the importance of touch in Jesus' ministry – he touches, or allows himself to be touched by, the very people who would make him ritually unclean in "religious" terms; a menstruating woman; a leper; a prostitute; a dead girl. True religion lies in his intimate involvement with the reality of their lives – a reality which can be hard and unpleasant, and doesn't shy away from the fact of sex.

Jesus and the Pharisees are about two totally different sorts of religion. The one is about life, about finding yourself, about God-with-us. The other is not really religion at all, but moralism. Listen to the voice of the Church; how often does it seem to consist of people laying down the law? This is bad: that is good. Power; rules; judgement. They can peel laws out of the Bible at the drop of a hat, conveniently forgetting that the Bible is about relationship with God, not a code of morality at all.

The second set of voices are the Rentacrowd, that Mark introduces throughout the gospel; sometimes more like extras in a play than real people. They come and go, without our really understanding what they are doing, or what they are thinking. Sometimes they are positive about Jesus, marvelling at what they see. At one point, Jesus has to escape into a boat; the crowd are so eager to get what they can out of him (power? healing? magic?) that there is a danger that they will crush him in the process. At other times they are critical; when Jesus goes to revive Jairus' daughter, they jeer at him. When the blind man Bartimaeus cries out to Jesus for help, they try to shut him up. In the end, they come to ridicule the dying Jesus.

Perhaps the warning here is that if we turn the group into a golden calf, we will not be able to see what Jesus is about either. There is an intense relief at being able to shed individual responsibility. You can see it in churches and football grounds, in Nazi rallies and political meetings, in discos and in war. There is that strange phrase "I enjoyed it, because it took me out of myself". The crowd can "ooh!" and "aahh" at Jesus; rush him for what they may be able to get out of him; welcome him in triumph into Jerusalem; but in the end, they are no nearer understanding him. In a sense, they cannot see the reality of him, precisely because they have been taken out of themselves. In order to meet him at a real level, they need to be very firmly centred in the reality of themselves as individuals.

In an interview, a German man described what it was like to be present at one of Hitler's mass rallies in the thirties. All around him people were laughing and crying, shouting and singing, buoyed up by the most intense feelings of joy and purpose. All he could feel was a desolating sense of loneliness. He longed to be able to believe; something inside him urged him to make the leap of faith, to share the joy, to lose his isolation. But he could not surrender his identity. Like an atheist stranded at a revivalist meeting, he had to stand there and weep for his own loneliness, and weep for what was being done to the many.

And do we find our identity in the crowd? Sometimes it is argued that it is wrong to emphasize the individual, at the expense of the group. Perhaps this argument would bear more weight if the societies which employ it did not seem to use it as a way of exercising control over the many. The concept of the individual – of the vital and unique importance of each single human being – is one that holds all groups and all political systems under judgement. In the end, the group is part of what destroys Jesus; but at what a cost; and what are the values they are left with?

But if we need to be wary of religion and of the voice of the many, surely we can trust those closer to us? Mark's gospel isn't so sure. When you get to family and friends, the pressure to hang on to idealistic myths is particularly strong. Somewhere there is a perfect mother, who never feels anger and never longs for the days when her life wasn't cluttered by children. Somewhere there is a perfect wife or husband, who never gets annoyed or sulky, and who never gets overpowered by intense feelings of anger towards their spouse. But that doesn't sound like Jesus' family. For Mark, they are apparently so unimportant as hardly to merit a mention, but when they do appear, they are highly unsympathetic to Jesus. We first hear of them when we are told that they wanted to have him taken in charge, because they thought he was mad. Shortly afterwards, his mother and brothers arrive outside the place where he is having a meeting, and send in a rather peremptory message telling him to come out. (Please don't ask about the brothers; they are there in the text, and you can only explain them away by inventing stories outside the text like adoption, half-brothers, etc. The theory of the perpetual virginity of Mary hadn't been heard of when the gospel was written. Anyway, why is it so important to us that this ultimate mother figure should be sexually untouched? Is there something wrong or dirty about sex?)

And that's all we hear about the family. Later, Jesus goes back to his home town, and is unable to work any miracles; "after all", say the people, "it's only Jesus the carpenter. We know his mother and brothers and sisters well. What's special about him?"

We are so pressured by the myths of normality and perfection, that we feel ourselves constantly held up to judgement. The Holy Family could not possibly be anything but perfect. Other people's marriages work better. Other mothers never hit their kids. And yet . . . A couple in their nineties were interviewed on their seventieth wedding anniversary. The reporters gushed in a slushy, romantic, patronizing way. "Oh ho ho", roguishly, "and have you ever thought of divorce?" The question was expecting a resounding NO. You could almost hear the violins playing in the background. "Divorce?", said the old lady, with an astonished look, "Never!" But before the reporters could sigh collectively about the wondrous joys of married life, she added firmly, "Murder, often!"

Why shouldn't Jesus have been on bad terms with his family? Perhaps they were going through a bad patch. Perhaps, more likely, he belonged to a perfectly normal human family, with perfectly normal human emotions, and all the rows and laughter and sulks and smiles that go into being normal. Somehow, somewhere, we have got hooked on this sickly-sweet ideal of what it means to be a "nice" human, and the reality of what we are has been left far behind. And oh! the guilt we suffer as a result. What a relief to consider at least the possibility that Jesus' home life was not a bed of (artificial) roses. Once again, there is a golden calf of unreality in human relationships, and the more difficult path of finding God in the ups and downs and storms and stillnesses of real life. "Marriages", said a friend, "aren't made in heaven. They are made at the kitchen table on bleak mornings. They are made in beds cold with argument. And they are made in the bitter-sweet knowledge that the familiar face on the other side of the room may conceal a million imperfections, and yet that that face knows you, and stands between you and emptiness." Amen to that.

What little we see of Jesus' family suggests that they found his chosen life to be very hard for them to accept or understand. If you look at the disciples, they don't appear to be much better. This may be particularly hard for us to grasp, because we have been brought up on a diet of "saint = perfect". Once again, there's a massive golden calf erected to the idea that some people are perfect, and others (you and me) very definitely aren't. The ideal, it seems, is to be less than human; we are left to pick up the messy bits and pieces of our lives, whilst somewhere there exists a master race who don't sulk, make mistakes, make love, go to the loo, laugh or cry.

In a terrifying experiment, a teacher told her class that all children with blue eyes were racially inferior to other children. They were less intelligent, had unpleasant personal habits, were lazy, and could not be trusted. All the children in her class with blue eyes were made to wear a special sign. Hidden cameras filmed the result. Within a few hours, the blue-eyed children *were* less intelligent; they became furtive and listless, and the other children began to treat them with contempt. The point of the experiment was to show that if we are expected to be or behave in a certain way, then the odds are that we will become what we are thought to be. Its particular application was to show what happens to black people in a white culture. The danger is that it may also show what happens to humans in a "religious" culture. Being human is somehow less than enough; other people are always far more wonderful – especially if they have been dead for several hundred years.

Mark's story has little time for such an idea. To put it kindly, the disciples are a washout as far as being supportive or understanding of Jesus. Time after time after time, they fail to understand what he is about, so much so that Jesus has an affectionate(?) nickname for them – "little-faiths". The main problem is that they are completely unwilling or unable to take on board what Jesus sees as the key to his ministry: the need to follow the dangerous path of sacrificial love. He tells them about his imminent death, and their reaction is to get involved in an argument amongst themselves about status. He tells them again, and Peter grabs him and starts to give him a real dressing down. After the first miracle of the loaves, they are faced with another hungry crowd to feed, "Oh how on earth are you going to do that?" they moan, as if they'd learned nothing from the first miracle. From there they go straight on to a boat. "Oh, we haven't got any bread to eat", they whinge – and yet here they are on a boat with a man who has just provided enough bread to feed thousands of people.

But of course the great betrayal comes at the end. They are unable to watch with Christ as he waits in terror and agony for what is to happen to him. When the arrest comes, they all run away . . . so much for dreams of power and status. Peter denies knowing him, and when the crucifixion comes, the disciples are nowhere to be found. Perhaps new disciples have been found: a group of women watch with Jesus as he dies. Then three women are brave enough to go to anoint his body on the Sunday morning. The men? Well, the men have vanished, and it is to the women that the message of fear and hope is entrusted: "He has risen; he is not here."

If there is any meaning at all to the word "saint", it may be that it describes people who are more, not less, human. Jesus chose these people; they were his friends. They may have been pretty useless as golden calves, but they were certainly human. Their voice has to be taken seriously. After all, where is the perfect friend who understands everything that we think or say or do? Where is the perfect friend who doesn't get cross, or badger us, or lean on us, or see through us? Friendship, human love, is such a precious gift in our lives (a gift so precious that it deserves all the hard work to keep it in order), that any pseudo-religious concept of perfectible humanity is a profound insult. What we have to deal with is people, complex ambiguous people. Religion/God/meaning is in and through those people. Making false idols of saints or "perfect" human beings is just a distraction from the task of loving the reality of humanity; and, I suspect, a distraction from having to face up to the reality of our own humanity.

All these voices, family, religion, the crowd, the friends, circle around the mysterious figure of Jesus; each one trying to push him in a certain direction. But he is not to be pushed. Nor will Mark's story let us push him, even though the temptation to make the biggest golden calf of all is strong in us. All through the story, Jesus refuses to define himself. No sooner have people made an advance in understanding, than he commands them to be silent. People ask for a sign, but he will not give it; they want to know what is the source of his authority, but he will not tell them. He is a figure full of anger and compassion. Somehow it doesn't seem to carry over into English translations, but in the original Greek he is a stormy character, ablaze with emotion at human suffering and wilful blindness.

As golden calf builders, we long to be able to get a very firm grip on this enigmatic character. This is God; this is perfect man. But somehow Jesus eludes us. His meaning is woven into the story, and cannot be extracted without our losing hold of him and substituting an idol – an idol that is probably waiting, ready programmed into our computers.

Just to keep the programming at bay, perhaps we should look at one or two places where the story warns us about adopting easy answers. The first is in chapter 8, where Jesus asks the disciples who people think he is. "John the Baptist, or Elijah, or one of the prophets", comes the answer. "And you," he asks, "who do you say I am?" Is it possible that Jesus genuinely wants to know what they think, because he is uncertain what his role is to be? Being completely human, how could he be certain about such a thing? Isn't it through throwing questions around with our friends or family, that we come to new understanding? Peter answers, "You are the Messiah", but Jesus neither agrees nor disagrees; instead he swears the disciples to silence about himself, almost in rebuke. Then he goes on to talk about the inevitable suffering that awaits the "son of man". (As we've seen before, "son of man" is a very ambiguous term, which could simply mean "one", or could mean a lot more.)

All through the gospel, various titles are applied or almost applied to Jesus, and then are immediately snatched back and redefined in terms of suffering. It is as if Mark is saying that you can only understand what these labels mean if you look at them in the context of the story. If you take out a label and try to use it on its own, it will be meaningless. In chapter 10, a young man runs up to Jesus and calls him "Good Teacher". "Why do you call me good?" answers Jesus. "No one is good but God alone." Is it possible that Jesus is even rejecting the label "sinless" that we long to hang around his neck? Certainly he could be mistaken. He may well have believed that God would intervene in history soon after his death; there is even the possibility that he thought he might be the forerunner of the one who would bring the end. Perhaps it isn't so hard for us to imagine that he might be wrong; but to be capable of sin. . . .

If we are going to be honest with the story, and not manipulate it, then that possibility is at least there. And perhaps it is an important possibility. What would it mean to have a human being who was incapable of negativity or sin, and whose thoughts were always and only sweetness and light? Such a being would be so far from our own experience and understanding, that we might have to ask whether they were human at all. Could we communicate with someone who had no experience of boiling with rage, or longing for another human being? How could they possibly understand what we were talking about, unless they had experienced it for themselves? We can stand in the zoo and speculate about what the lions are thinking, but it is impossible that we would ever know unless we were able to become lions ourselves.

Father Borelli, who lived and worked with the urchins in the Naples slums, had to live their life to the full before he could understand them or win their trust. And that meant that he had to join them in stealing. If someone was only capable of being good, or had lived a life where they had only done/thought/dreamed the good, it would be impossible for them to understand how it feels to be human. Borelli could only understand the kids by living their life with them, otherwise he would just have been an interested spectator from outside. Unless someone has actually experienced what it is to hate, lust, lie, sulk, cheat, and so on, they can only have a sort of theoretical concept of what these things may be; they have no common experience of what it means to be human, on which they might draw when they want to understand people or to communicate with them. If you said to such a person, "I hate Bill", they could only guess at what you meant; in the same way, if they had never tasted cheese, it would be meaningless to tell them "this omelette tastes cheesy".

Perhaps this brings us to one of the most central episodes in the story. Before his ministry can begin, Jesus is driven into the desert by the Spirit, and is tempted by Satan for forty days and nights. What form the temptation took, Mark doesn't tell us. Matthew and Luke suggest that it was to do with easy ways of gaining power and authority. There is also a strong element in their stories of "let yourself be taken care of" – "you can have bread, if you want it; or a kingdom if you let me take charge; or why not let go, and let the angels take care of you . . .?" Mark gives us nothing specific as a temptation; but perhaps "nothing" is the key to the temptation. Jesus is totally alone, except for the extraordinary phrase "he was among the wild beasts".

When we are alone in a desert, be it in factory, office, suburb or bed, strange wild beasts can come crawling out of the rocks and caves of our imagination. Fantasies, illusions, seductions, perversions; strange creatures that have been hiding in the darkness, and that we have kept firmly pushed out of the way. Sometimes it is only in dreams that they prowl around us, but when we reach the desert they can be there in the daytime too. And perhaps the temptation is to try to blast them out of existence with the fire of our moral indignation. We are the golden calf; our gold must be of the purest. But these creatures are not from outside; they are part of us.

Mark adds, "and the angels waited on him". Is it possible

that the wild beasts and the angels are one and the same thing? The temptation is to make oneself a god; to reject all that goes to make up one's humanity, in pursuit of the terrible pride of being perfect. The temptation is to be a golden calf; with a perfect façade, but hollow inside, with no sign of life.

Right at the start of his ministry, Jesus has to ask himself who he is and what his goals are to be. We all have goals, and perhaps there are very large chunks of our personalities that we repress and rationalize and deceive ourselves and others about, in the name of those goals. In other words, we, or the pressures that others put on us, can maim or wound whole parts of ourselves. Perhaps the temptation for Jesus was to do the same; to reject many of the parts that made for his completeness – the wild beasts. Instead, perhaps he had the courage and the love to live with them; to accept them, and what they had to bring him – "and the angels waited on him".

"Love your neighbour AS YOURSELF", commanded Jesus. The question of the desert is, how much our pride or fear will let our love extend itself to the broken and ruined parts of ourselves. How much compassion can we have for all those weak, sick, disgusting, perverse, wounded wild beasts inside us? The desert asks how far we dare go in trying to build an inner society, based on the principle of love and compassion and hospitality. The less compassion we can find for ourselves, the less we will have for others.

Perhaps that is the secret of Jesus and the Pharisees. How could they have compassion, when half their being was battened down, feared and ignored? But Jesus' love could not be threatened by the "wild beasts" he found in others, because the desert experience had built a society of love in him, where even the most broken and wretched could find shelter and compassion. Is this why "Christian" smiles and niceness can sometimes seem so cold and threatening, so superficial and unreal? They are like vault doors, clamped shut over the chaos behind – a whole world of wild beasts, unloved and unacknowledged. And the fear that at any moment, the chaos might break through; no wonder the mess and ambiguity of the world is regarded with such fear; or that certain classes of sinner (usually sexual) are regarded with such horror and disgust.

People feel embarrassed about their humanity when they are forced to go into church for baptisms, weddings and funerals. The braver ones are openly hostile, the others behave unnaturally, afraid of putting a foot wrong. Perhaps part of the reason for their being so ill at ease is that they can sense, under the hearty smiles of the vicar and the crocodile grins of the regular congregation, a deep blast of hatred being aimed in their direction. Their normal and noisy humanity, with the odd wild beast poking its nose out, has set all the vault doors straining, and the religious programmes whirring into overdrive. Of course we can't love these people; we ache to convert them; to get our hands on them, and smash everything about them that sets such worrying tremors going in our hidden, unloved, unaccepted wilderness.

The usual answer to any demand for compassion for these wild beasts inside us, is to say "Oh, and I suppose you think we should all go around raping people, and stealing and murdering . . ." But the beasts only have power when they are unloved and unacknowledged. If we reject these parts of ourselves, they don't go away – they *can't* go away, even if they wanted to, because they are part of the reality of us. If we lock them away, then heaven help the person we meet who reminds us of them; our urge will be to destroy them.

The holiday route to Devon was busy with bank holiday traffic. Father stopped the car at a lay-by, and asked his wife and three little kids to wait while he went for a pee. Ten minutes passed, and then to the wife's horror, she saw her husband being escorted out of the public lavatory by two policemen. This good, hard-working, family man had tried to grope another man; the wild beast that he had denied for so long had burst out of its confinement. And the police who had volunteered to hang around in the lavatory, and who roughed him up a little, what beasts inside themselves were they punishing in the shape of this man?

The desert experience leads to a deep humility, because we don't want to be lumbered with all these shadowy figures. Many of them are not very pleasant or socially acceptable. They remind us too vividly that we can never be a glorious golden calf, but are condemned to the reality of being a strange mixture of muck and glory. Part of being the donkey is to accept that donkeys are messy, smelly, stubborn, bad-tempered, fairly ugly, and may have a ration of fleas. That is not all there is to the donkey, as we have seen, but it is part of the package. Humility comes from learning to love all the nasty bits. Humility, and comedy – because who can take themselves totally seriously, when they know that there is a complete circus of wild beasts dancing around inside them?

We have said many times that the prophet needs the donkey. But the donkey needs the prophet too. We need a joyful and comic acceptance of all the humiliating parts of ourselves; we will carry them with us wherever we go, and we must learn to care for them. But we also need the prophet voice to remind us that caring does not mean indulging. There is a moral dimension to our lives, and we must be quite clear that some parts of ourselves are a burden, not to be tolerated. The prophet will demand change, and will want to judge harshly; the donkey will soldier on in a comic, joyful way. They both need each other; either one taken alone is wrong. The comic double act judges and accepts; when it is in balance, then perhaps the wild beasts really can become angels.

I have made much of Christ in the desert, because that experience is one that we all must face if we are ever to be able to give a truthful answer to the question "Who am I?" It began his ministry, and all that came after was only possible because of that rootedness in the reality of his own humanity. But as well as having a compassionate society within ourselves, we also need to be part of a compassionate framework – we need others. There are many golden calves erected in this area, often called "Walk Tall" or "Be Strong". The myth is that we shouldn't need other people, and that we should have a deep inner strength and toughness which will get us through anything. It is certainly true that if we haven't got that inner society, we will need others in a clinging sort of way. So many parts of our identity will be missing or unacknowledged, that we will rush to fill the gap with what we can suck from others. But the "Rambo" toughness of being strong and refusing to accept weakness or need in oneself, is really only another version of that incompleteness. If you feel the vacuum inside, you either rush to fill it up with what you can get from other people, or else you deny that emptiness with all the strength at your disposal. "I don't need anybody" really means "Mummy, I'm scared".

But if Jesus had befriended all the parts of himself, then he was able to accept need and weakness when it came. You cannot overstate the strength of the words that Mark uses to describe the torment that Jesus goes through in the Garden of Gethsemane. "Horror and dismay" sound so feeble to us in English. So does "My heart is ready to break with grief". Somehow the words in the original Greek have overtones of that feeling you may have experienced when your mind can no longer cope with what is happening; you feel as if the pressure of emotion may quite literally blow the top of your head off. Perhaps, as we were trying to say before, such words can only mean something to us if we have experienced something similar for ourselves. If you have watched someone you love very much dying, I think you will understand what I am trying to say. There is grief and horror as a theoretical concept; and then there is grief and horror as the real thing. Unless someone has experienced them, they cannot know what you are talking about.

In this need, Christ turns to his friends. He needs them; he feels he cannot get through it without them. And, poor old things, they let him down. He is forced to go through it alone, just as so many of us, in the end, have to go through it alone. Then the trial, the beating, the tormenting, the questioning, and finally that terrible cry from the cross, "My God, my God, why have you forsaken me?".

People have tried to argue away the awfulness of that cry. "He's quoting from a psalm, and of course the psalm ends happily, so what he's really doing is praising God", they say. But that isn't what the story gives us. What does it mean to die alone, doubting everything that you have done or been, and doubting the value of everything that you have put your trust in? This really is the final agony of mankind — bring down the curtain, the comedy is finished; and that is all it was, the whole of my life, all the hope and love and pain, just something that was good for a laugh. The rest is silence.

The story ends very soon after that. The women go to anoint the dead body of the man who died in despair. But his tomb is empty. He has risen? They run away in terror. End of story.

And what is the meaning of all that? And where was God? And what difference, if any, does this make to our lives? The answers must be the same that we gave to *The Wind in the Willows*. There is something too precious and important here to be entrusted to the theoreticians. If they want to argue about the existence or otherwise of God, let them get on with it. If they want to build elaborate structures around

Jesus, let them get on with mummifying him. (Perhaps it is fortunate that the tomb is empty, so that religious people cannot get their hands on him.) But we want to trust the story; to live with it, and grow with it, and let it come into a dance with our lives. In some strange way, through the telling and retelling of the history of the man Jesus, we come to affirm our own history — our own past, present, and future. Because of his story, there is no human path that we may be called to follow, however mucky or desolate, that has not already been sanctified.

Because we want to say something "more" about him, we will be forced to use God language, and strange words that may sound wild and unfamiliar to anyone leading a profoundly boring and logical life: words like "new life", "resurrection", "redemption". We are forced to use language in order to talk about what the story means to us. But we are in danger if we start thinking that the words have a life of their own. The donkey sees God in the complexity of reality. The systematic ambiguity of the story safeguards us from making golden calves. What we have is the story. We also have our own story. The two ambiguities, the two complexities, the two realities — as they join in the dance together, the stories come to explain each other; one brings light to the other. As the Jew may come to understand his own story by telling the story of the Exodus, so we will tell the story of Jesus, and in doing so, come to take our own story more seriously. Somewhere in all this, God is at work. For the moment, we cannot know more than that. But when we can learn to trust the stories, to stop controlling them and start living them, then, perhaps, we shall begin to understand.

7

The Fearful Unbelief

One blustery March day, a man was walking along the cliffs at Beachy Head. A strong gust of wind hit him, and blew him over the edge. For a few nightmare seconds he fell, and then as luck would have it, he managed to grab hold of a little sapling, growing out of the cliff face. For what seemed an eternity, he hung there screaming for help: "Help! Help! For God's sake, someone help me! Is there anyone there?" But answer came there none. "Is there anyone there?", he cried desperately, as his hold became weaker. Suddenly a voice answered him, "I am here. What do you want?" "I don't know. Just help me. Save me. SAVE ME." "Very well," answered the voice, "but if I am to save you, you must trust me." "I trust you. I trust you", came the anguished squeak. "Very good", said the voice. "This is God speaking, and if I am to save you, all you have to do is to let go of the sapling and fall. When you fall, I will catch you and bring you safely to ground. Now just let go." There was a very long pause, and then came a sad little cry, "Is there anyone else there?"

Well, under the circumstances, who could blame him? Perhaps we have all experienced that feeling of the ground giving way under our feet — either literally, or metaphorically. Very early on in my job as a priest (about ten days out of theological college, actually), I had to spend a lot of time with a man who had lost most of his jaw in an operation for cancer. It was very hard to understand what he was trying to say, and matters weren't made any easier for him by the fact that he had an almost constant flow of pus/saliva/phlegm, which he had to spit out into a bowl that he held in front of him. The smell was terrible.

There was so much emotion buzzing around in that little hospital room. He was frightened, ashamed, shocked, felt like a leper, and angry with me for being so slow to understand him. I felt sick, unable to cope, and wished I could be a hundred miles away. In desperation, I clung on to the certainties: God is love (and has lovingly created cancer?); I am a priest (and about as much use to this suffering man as a used bandage); I can pray for him and give him my blessing (at least that will shut him up for a minute, and leave me in control of the situation); all will be well in the light of eternity (but does that mean that what is happening in this room isn't real — that the truth is somewhere in a text book in an Oxford college?)

As long as I clung on to my certainties, we were like two strangers. The reality of what was going on between us, and the reality of the fact of death that was staring us in the face, went ignored. I think it was after I'd excused myself for about the fourth time ("Must just pop out to the loo", I lied glibly, as I rushed out of the room to throw up), that I thought "This is ridiculous". If there was any reality at all in what was happening, and if there was any reality in the idea of God, then it was contained in that room; in the approaching death of a man being put through a terrible ordeal, in the emotions of two frightened and bewildered people, even in the reality of that sick-making surgical bowl.

And so I let go. Slowly we built up a way of communicating, so that we could explore what was happening and finally dare to confront the awfulness of the present, and the fear of the future. We were travelling over uncharted ground for both of us, and sometimes it felt as if we were falling into deep shadowy chasms where none of the old answers could say anything to us. We spoke of disgust and fear and the loneliness of dying — all the most terrifying brute beasts that the desert could throw at us. And yet by walking together among the beasts – by allowing ourselves to fall – somehow the beasts became tamer. They would still be fearful, and it would be hard to love them, but somehow they became ours ... they belonged to us, instead of being nightmare demons thrown at us by some alien force from outside. We learned that we could let go and fall, and yet that after the fall we could also rise again.

And we spoke of beautiful things. Of his life, all that he had done and been; the hopes he had never realized. Together we listened to his story. We were in a modern hospital room, but sometimes it might almost have been as if we were alone in the desert together, sitting round a fire, telling and retelling this story. And slowly all the wild beasts were drawn to the warmth of the fire, and gathered round to become part of the story. We could include them all; all were important and real, because all affirmed the central importance and reality of this man and his story. I think the ravaged remains of his face were one of the most terrible things I have ever seen. In the firelight, in the falling and rising together, he was beautiful.

If I were to use risky language, I would have to say that at first I thought I was bringing God to a suffering man. In fact, all I had brought was a book of words and my own refusal to face up to reality. "God" was already there; was there in the failure and the anger; in a frightened curate throwing up in a hospital gents; was there in the realities of both our stories, and our growing awareness and acceptance of those realities; was there in the strange journey that we undertook together. God was the journey?

And there was a third story that we told. After we had made our stories our own, we began to find that another story was playing around in our minds; the story of the life and death of the man we looked at in the last chapter. No longer a resource book for frightened curates, the Gospel became a new voice for us – the three stories came into a gentle dance together. Death, fear, hope, joy, amazement . . . once we had stopped trying to use the story of Jesus as a pain-reliever, controlling the dosage, it took on a life of its own. In the light of our own stories, we could see it more clearly; and by its light, we could see our own stories more clearly.

Letting go or control; the donkey or the prophet. All through this book, we have seen how heavily the cards are stacked in the prophet's favour. He has all the voices on his side, and all the voices have been to do with control. But if we let the prophet steer us, it is not we who are in control of our lives; it is not our own reality that we are living, but someone else's reality. Culture, parents, state, system, religion – we cling on desperately, to stop ourselves from falling. And the void we dread falling into is reality. We have learned that it is dangerous or unacceptable to be ourselves, so that reality is barred to us. We have learned that life is risky and ambiguous, so we cling on to something, anything, that will save us from falling headlong into it.

But perhaps the time comes for all of us, when we have to ask what sort of a life it is we are living, when the main object seems to be to hang on like grim death to a crumbling cliff face. Have we really dedicated our whole lives to living up to what others expect of us? All that energy gone into playing a part, trying to breathe life into an acceptable shopwindow dummy? That sapling we cling to is called "you should . . ." For safety, for security, in order to be looked after, in order not to be alone on the cliff face, we struggle to be what others think we should be (and the others include the many voices of the prophet inside us), and never dare risk the fall of becoming who we really *are*.

And our attitude to ourselves is one of power and control. Our society is all about "having". We have things. Things are fixed and describable. One of the things we have is

110

ourselves. For the prophet to remain in control, our very personalities, and those of others, must be fixed and describable – actors in a play, labels, machines. But the process of being human is much more complex than that. You can give a neat description of a mask or a role, but not of human experience.

Prophets are big on knowledge. They "have" knowledge as a possession; it is one of the things that makes them feel secure. But there is another sort of knowledge which is to do with being able to see more clearly, to know more deeply. How can we "know" reality? We cannot define it, or encompass it intellectually. Only something greater than reality could do that. But we can work to make ourselves sensitive to it – we can attune ourselves to it. But this means a loss of control; reality is reality; a rose is a rose is a rose – like humble but excited children, we need to attune ourselves to what is really before us. Not what we think should be there; not what others tell us we ought to see there; but what is really there. Alas, the more firmly fixed we are in playing the prophet, the more desperately we cling to our persona, the thing about ourselves we can "have", the less we will see.

It is the donkey who knows. And it is the donkey we need to listen to, even though it will mean letting go of all our certainties. But how much we hate the donkey! So much of organized religion is made up of people hanging on to the cliff face. Their whole personalities are frozen with the effort – they are rigid, and dare not move for fear of falling. For them, God is the sapling. The least movement of its leaves, and they are thrown into a panic. No wonder they react with fury to anyone who tries to loosen their hold. As long as they can cling on, they are in control of their lives – just. And the fall? Well, it could be fear of death, the pressures of reality, or it could just be the fear of falling into the reality of oneself . . . that you would drop through the void and discover that instead of being the ideal golden calf you long to be, you are part of a comic double-act, with a large and stroppy donkey. For many of us "religious" people, that would be the equivalent of being dashed onto the rocks. And so we desperately look for proof; proof that the sapling is big and strong and powerful. There is a very worrying trend in the Church at the moment to create or sustain belief in the sapling by asking it to perform mighty deeds; "a miracle" we cry, with unashamed relief that the thing really works; "packed churches, loads of converts" – see, we're not mad after all; "gifts of the Spirit", etc., etc. Of course, we have conveniently to forget that further along the cliff there are all sorts of other saplings fulfilling exactly the same functions for those of other faiths, or of none. There are even saplings called "therapy" or "cocaine". Once you are hanging on to the thing, whatever it is, you have GOT to believe in it – it is all there is between you and destruction.

There was a recent court case about a businessman who had effectively surrendered control of his life to a hypnotherapist. A successful man, he had allowed his life to be dominated by someone to whom he gave his complete trust, and, so said the prosecution, much of his money. Those of us who are on the cliff face NEED powerful leaders to reassure us. What on earth are we saying, when tens of thousands of people turn out to idolize another human being? The Pope, TV evangelists, the Ayatollahs, our wonderful vicar . . . we gladly, even ecstatically, surrender the complexity of our adulthood in order to become reassured children again. And like crooked hypnotists, they will strip us of the riches of our humanity. Just listen to some of these so-called "religious" leaders talking; they are like waxwork models of the Parent; calm, confident, all-knowing, laying down the law – is there anything for which they don't have an answer?

And if, by chance, one of them should dare to suggest that

he doesn't know, or should try to persuade people to make up their own minds or assume responsibility for their own lives, just watch how the people will turn and rend him. Talk to a few clergy who have dared to ask the children to grow up, and see what their congregations have done to them. On the cliff face, we demand certain qualities in our leaders; if they are to save us from falling, they must be strong/confident/reassuring/certain/powerful . . a subtle cocktail of all that the Prophet-Parent-cultural tapes demand. And as the world gets more and more complex, and there is an increasing sense of our not being able to be in control of our own lives, so we will turn to these powerful figures and invest them with more and more authority. Who wants to die alone and desolate on a cross, when you can have a High Priest to tell you what to do?

It was Carlyle who said, "Alas, the fearful Unbelief is unbelief in yourself". To tell a "religious" person that the sapling is not only unimportant, but a positive bar to life, is sacrilegious unbelief. If only we dared listen to the donkey, who could tell us that we are not worshipping God, but a pseudo-divine safety harness. But we cannot believe the donkey, because that would mean believing in ourselves. And we know from all our programming, that we are not reliable witnesses. It is a vicious circle: we cannot trust ourselves, because we have been told that we are not trustworthy. Like convicts in a chain gang, we walk round and round in circles, dragging the ball and chain of our religion. People who have managed to escape look at us with pity or horror; what they know, but what we dare not accept, is that we carry the keys to our own chains; our captors are in our own heads. But being free is frightening, because then we would have to take responsibility for our own lives. We would rather spend our lives clinging on to certainty, than risk free fall. We will make a golden calf of another human being, and gladly hand over the keys of our freedom, as long as they promise to keep us safely impris-oned. Just watch – it is happening in religion and politics all over the world. Who would you like to be your gaoler?

The donkey, of course, would tell us too that while we are spending our lives walking round and round in circles, or staring fixedly at the rock face, we are unlikely to see God. That may not matter very much to us, because we are only interested in God for what we can get out of Him, and a god you can hold on to is much more use than a God who involves risk. If God is the fall into reality, then we will shout very loudly, "IS THERE ANYONE ELSE THERE?"

In her efforts to make the prophet see, the donkey crushed his foot against a wall. There are religious people who can see very clearly, and it is always because they have been hurt or damaged in some way. There are moments when the prophet drops his guard, and we can feel the donkey lying down under us, or hurting us. It may be something actually physical – we get ill, our backs play up, we have "accidents". It may be something less tangible; we find it hard to sleep, we get depressed, moody, or irritable for no apparent reason, or else the whole business of living be-comes such a hard slog, and it is hard to find a reason for anything. Or perhaps our dreams and fantasies start to trouble us. When the prophet wakes up in the morning he says, "What a terrible dream!", and promptly tries to forget it. The dreams and fantasies are somehow out of his control, so he must not admit that they have a reality of their own – they are intruders from outside, to be frowned upon and forgotten. In dreams we say that we have been taken out of ourselves; but in fact we have been let into ourselves; for a moment there has been a chink in the armour of our assumed personality – the donkey has spoken to us in strange poetic images.

Dreams are the one part of our lives over which we have no control, and perhaps that is why we mistrust them so much. Strange figures come and go. The beasts assume identities, and then fade away. We can try to take control by ignoring them, or saying they come from the devil. We can try to manipulate them with clever interpretations, all aimed at increasing our control over our conscious and unconscious selves. Or we can try to make friends of them; they are the lost children circling around our house, begging to be invited in. They are all the parts of ourselves that we are frightened to own, and that we must re-own if we are to be complete.

When it comes to dreams and fantasies, it is terribly important to be sure that we don't let the prophet take over. He will not be interested in befriending the dream, but in using it to increase his power. The same may be true with our fantasies. There is a welcome trend in the Church of England at the moment, to explore the values of Ignatian spirituality. Now anything that will help in the hard slog of prayer is all for the good, and the fact that Ignatian spirituality actually acknowledges the fact that we have fantasies is a relief. But when it comes to what they ask you to do with them, warning bells begin to sound. In effect, you are asked to exercise control over them – to point them towards God. As always with prayer, the proof of the pudding lies in the eating – anything that increases our capacity to live honestly and with an open, accepting love towards all people, must be said to "work". But my fear is that the prophet voice can always put his ungodly programming into Godly terms. If we are not careful, we may find that this is just another form of the prophet wrenching at the reins, trying to turn the donkey in the direction that he feels she ought to go. Spiritual "exercises", "retreat" – they are all military terms. If they work to build up the prophet's power over the donkey, we may find, yet again, that we will be chasing unreal gods, and ignoring what the donkey has to tell us.

Sometimes dreams are like the donkey trying to remind us

of our story; telling us to concentrate on what is happening in our lives, and what has brought us here. But if we are clinging to the cliff face, we prefer not to think about the present. We think about the past – how nice it was when . . . (the Garden of Eden?) – and we think about the future – how nice it would be if . . . (heaven?). Some of us spend most of our time in the past or the future. We rehearse the things that will happen – what I will say to X, what I will do if Y happens; and we recreate the past: what I really meant to say to X (and, in time, that will be the way I remember it), how I won the battle of Y (actually, it was a massacre). We find it almost impossible to be in the present moment . . . think of all those time-saving gadgets, and rushing home early from work in order to have more time to . . . to forget oneself in front of the latest episode of "Eastenders".

You may have wondered why I concentrated on some of the most painful aspects of Jesus' ministry in the last chapter. I was trying to show that if we are going to be honest with the story, and not try to interfere for our own ends, then it will be made up of a myriad different colours – a kaleidoscope of emotions, events, feelings, voices, images, all of which must be allowed to play their part. It is the same with our own stories. We need to see what is happening *now*; what the process is inside us and around us; what is the actual feeling, touching, seeing, moving, doing. It would not be too strong to say that we live under a curse; the curse is the ideal – the ideal human should be. . . . the ideal you should be . . . But the ideal is a fantasy concocted by terrified people hanging on by their finger nails. Real knowledge means being dis-illusioned – getting rid of the fantasy, and trying hard to see the reality.

Jung spoke of trying "to kindle a light in the darkness of mere being". How many of us feel that we are merely alive? Sleeping pills and Valium help for a bit, as does speaking in tongues, miraculous healing, the odd revivalist meeting, and queer-bashing. But the religious task is to kindle a light, not to hang on. (I'm sorry to sound so negative, but could you please explain to me what possible good it does to have a wonderful meeting where Mrs X is spiritually healed, or people jump up and down speaking gibberish, except as a most self-indulgent form of spiritual luxury? This is the Fortnum and Mason of religion, for the privileged few. Meantime, how many million people are dying of starvation, AIDS, war, religious or political bigotry?) Hanging-on religion is about trying to make yourself as comfortable as possible, justifying, glorifying and feeling good about a rather precarious sapling. Kindling a light means letting go. Perhaps it means taking the risk of lighting that warm, hospitable camp-fire in the desert, and waiting for all the unloved wild beasts to assemble – letting them share the warmth of the flame of love.

And kindling a light means caring for others – being involved in the human enterprise; perhaps bringing warmth; perhaps sending reassuring signals to those others who find the journey so bewildering, and who question the way we are asked to put so much effort into winning power, possessions or money, and how little effort we put into love, our humanity, and simply being alive. The novelist E. M. Forster said, "The greater the darkness, the brighter shine the little lights, reassuring one another, signalling: 'Well, at all events, I'm still here. I don't like it very much, but how are you?'." We try to find the light of meaning in the darkness of mere existence; and if we look around, we find that we are never alone in that quest.

Because all of life is a religious task. It is the strongest possible affirmation that what we are about is not mere being. The most annoying thing you can say to a vicar is, "Sorry you won't see me much in church, padre. I worship God on the golf course." And perhaps you do, far more effectively than you would do in church. Church can positively disable people from worship, because it can be about hanging on, guarding the deposit, not about letting go. Moses is called from the safe known to the unsafe unknown. Jesus has to leave his uncomprehending (safe) family. We too are called on pilgrimage, which means leaving the safe masks, labels and computers behind. (And possibly putting a gag on the prophet.)

In the past, perhaps the opening of vision came within a specifically religious context. Now, perhaps the artists, the lovers, the poets and the playwrights have taken over the torch. Time and again opinion polls come out showing that the bulk of the population believe in God, in some way or another. And time and again, they say that the Church has nothing to say to them. The exploring, the pilgrimage, the pushing out of the boundaries of what it means to be human, all this happens somewhere else. Except where it can gather together frightened people by promising them certainty, the Church is dying. It hangs on, but the lights are being kindled elsewhere. Even the scientists have more to say to us, as they study the physical world, or the human spirit, or the frontiers where the distinction between physical and spiritual seems to have disappeared. Sometimes the scientist feels something strike a responsive chord within him, as he struggles to understand the data given him; something in the outer material corresponds to some intimation of reality that he has felt within himself; he senses a unity undergirding himself and all things. He may even feel forced to start using god language.

But how do we start the exploring? Martin Buber asked what is the way we can follow if we are seeking the truth, and unity with God. His answer was that the way is like a road, but not a road we can walk along. Instead, it is a road that we are in the act of constructing. Straining with the effort, we roll the stones into place, and press them down. Then we laboriously roll the next one and the next one.

With great difficulty we smooth the surface and fill in the gaps and level it all off, so that it can be walked upon. So we cover a few yards; while we have been working, we have been on our way – the road, the way, has come into being under our feet. In other words, reality is not something separate from us to be reverenced and interpreted. Nor is God. Reality, truth, our relation to God, are part of the fabric of our lives.

Earlier, we looked at Kierkegaard's image of the man rowing a boat; it is only by concentrating on the reality of the NOW that he can undertake his journey. Albert Camus wrote about the myth of Sisyphus, the man who was punished by the gods by being condemned for ever to roll a giant boulder up a steep hill. When he reached the top, the boulder would roll downhill, and so his task would begin again. It is like the human story, said Camus, and yet you must imagine Sisyphus as being happy. At the moment when he reaches the top, before the boulder starts to roll down, he can know who he is and what he has done.

Somewhat more cheerful is the story of the man who was making a pilgrimage to Mecca. It was a long, difficult and dangerous journey with many hardships. Hungry and thirsty, battered by storms, in danger from brigands, the man stops and thinks to himself what an impossible journey he is making. He has suffered so much, and Mecca is still a long way away. Suddenly a light shines upon him, and a voice says, "Mecca is here. Mecca is now". The very road he is travelling, and the intensity of the longing he brings to his journey *are* the goal he is seeking.

Jewish thought is full of such stories. Like the rabbi from Warsaw who had a dream about finding a wonderful treasure, and searched for many years without finding anything. At last, exhausted and hopeless, he reached a strange city and stood leaning on a bridge, wondering what he could do. A stranger came up to him, and asked him what he was doing. The rabbi told him his story, and the man replied, "But how strange. I dreamed last night about a rabbi's house in Warsaw, and buried in the basement was the most wonderful treasure." The rabbi hurried home, and when finally he reached there, sure enough. . . .

If only we had the humility to shut up, for a change, and listen to what Jewish thinkers could tell us. Christianity has been in a position of cultural superiority for so long that its theology has become the voice of the bully or top-dog. It effortlessly adapts the social conventions of the particular culture where it finds itself, and becomes the voice of the social leaders. But these confident tones of the religious officer-class can begin to sound obscene in a world of complex and tragic suffering. The Jews understand what it means to be powerless and broken. Confronted by the Holocaust, they don't talk glibly about "forgiveness" or "resurrection"; if pushed, they may talk about the silence of God. Meaning isn't handed you on a plate; life questions us, and we work out the questions and the answers by our living. "God is within you" – that whole complex human process of suffering and death and powerlessness and joy and love and fear, is the place of meaning.

Perhaps in Christian terms we would say NOW is eternal life. The treasure we seek is here. The holy city, Jerusalem is HERE; Jerusalem is NOW. It is not a thing to be held, nor a doctrine to be believed. The way, the truth, the life, is in the quality of the being.

Are we brave enough to believe it? Can we let go, can the Church let go, and join the lovers, the artists, the comedians and the poets, and start to say wild, risky things about life? Have we condemned ourselves to staying forever grey, cold, bleak, clinging to the rock face? At the foot of Beachy Head, the pleasure boats come and go, full of holiday-makers, noisy and messy, and having a good time. Do they glance up the cliff to where the Church hangs, gradually becoming fossilized? What can a frozen Church say to people who are venturing on the sea of life, except shout for help, envy them, or invite them to come and join us on our miserable perch? God is below, waiting to catch us, but all our voices say "Don't let go", and so we shout our sermons into the wind. If we really wanted it, God could take us and put us with the people in the boat. We might get sea-sick, we might get wet, it might even be risky . . . but we would be with people, and we would be sharing their journey and making a journey of our own – we might even have a wonderful time. But do we really want to be with people, and dare we risk enjoying ourselves?

· "To kindle a light in the darkness of mere being." That is our task. To make friends with that comic warfare raging inside us. To listen to the prophet's many voices, and learn to recognize the tapes when they are playing. We can never get rid of them, but we must befriend them too – we can learn to carry them; they do not have to carry us. And to trust the donkey . . . she, more than anyone, will help us to be humble and to see things as they really are. To learn to tell our own story, listening to it in all its ambiguity and complexity, not trying to edit, expurgate, or rewrite.

If you are hanging from a cliff, and let go, you may be killed. If we let go control, trust and taste the reality of ourselves and others, then part of us may be killed too. It will be the controlling part that dies; the pretend me; the golden calf me that will shatter on the rocks. And frightened, naked, terribly vulnerable, perhaps we can start to learn what it means to be really human.

Kierkegaard calls it "to be that self which one truly is". If we risk the fall, certain things may happen to us. For a start, the person that we are *not*, the façade, will be broken on the rocks. At first, it will be very hard to say who we are. When we have stopped being ridden by other people's ideals ("I ought to be this . . . I ought to be that . . ."), when we have stopped living up to other people's expectations, when we have stopped trying to mould our behaviour into a form that we think will make other people like us, then we will have to start finding out what is really going on in our lives. (A simple example, but why is it such an enormous relief to be told that *all* parents have moments when they could gladly obliterate their baby? The curse of the ideal talks about the perfection of mother love. The reality of the intensity of anger one can feel for this screaming alien, is something else. The anger is real, and natural, and happening now – just as it happens to all parents. We can cope with the reality, hopefully, but what we can't cope with is the pressure of the unreal "oughts" , roles and façades. What a relief to be told that it's all right just to be what we are! And once we know that the anger is natural, once we can accept it in ourselves, then we rob it of half its power.)

Picking our way carefully along the foot of the cliff (I think the pleasure boat must come later . . .), other feelings come surging up. For a start, we can choose where we want to go, and that is an alarming prospect. Confidence will be slow to come, and we are bound to make mistakes. Walking barefoot over shingle, we may long for the comfort of the cliff face! But as we move on, we may begin to feel in touch with something strong inside us. The sea washes the shore, and ebbs and flows; the ground under our feet is sometimes warm, soft sand, sometimes wet, sometimes hard and painful. We discover that it is the same with our feelings; they change from day to day. They are not always consistent about people or events. (One moment I could cheerfully batter my baby; the next I feel an intensity of love that amazes me; the next I just feel tired. . . .) Kierkegaard again, "an existing individual is constantly in process of becoming" . . . we are all these different feelings and emotions; we can be all the richness and complexity of ourselves, without having to hide things from ourselves, or live in fear of the wild beasts.

After a while, we may even find that we are beginning to

enjoy the walk. Allowing ourselves to feel all the complexity inside us, we may begin to notice what is going on around us. The beauty of the sea, the sky, the air! A dolphin leaps from the water, a bird soars. At last, perhaps, we can listen to the child inside us, as it gasps with wonder at what it sees. Slowly, we begin to trust what we are feeling – to accept, to listen, to feel. We learn not to be afraid to BE all that we really are – good, bad, indifferent. And where before we were fixed, hating and fearing parts of ourselves, but unable to change them, we may find that by acccepting that we are a "process", change will come.

And reality no longer seems so threatening to us. Hanging from the cliff, issues seemed very clear cut; good/evil, black/white, safe/dangerous. But when you are on solid ground, you can see and accept that life is much more complex and ambiguous than that. When life is about holding on or falling, you feel alienated from the world around you – it feels dangerous, and the only good comes from those who help to tighten your grip. When you are free to walk through life, you find that it is made up of many rich and strange contrasts; there is meaning and beauty, and meaninglessness and ugliness. But because you no longer feel alienated from your surroundings, it is possible to accept reality – to feel a sense of kinship with the world around you.

Perhaps the time has come to join the other humans on the boat. An outraged voice may echo down from the cliff, "See, you got wet and dirty . . . I warned you" . . . but the time has come to leave the prophets hanging there. They have damaged us enough already. At first the other humans on the boat will feel very different from us; they each have their own thoughts and feelings and experiences. But that is no longer threatening; we can begin to value them for what they really are. And perhaps they can start to value us too. They may have lost that uneasy feeling when they are with us, that they are talking to a smiling mask. If we feel angry or jealous or hostile or sexy or lazy, they can cope with that, because they have the same emotions and they are all part of being human. What they can't cope with is the prophet mask which pretends to know and to be all sorts of wonderful things, and yet which covers a mess of unresolved and unaccepted humanity.

Has the prophet one last word of execration to hurl after us? Clinging to what he thinks he has control over, he may shout, "But this is humanism". To which we might reply that decent humanism – a concern for the human race and its responsibilities – is a lot healthier and a lot more useful than the sort of fixation he peddles as religion. But we'd want to say more than that, because all along we have been saying that the whole of human life is religious – human concerns are religious concerns. The story of Jesus is all about the claim that there is no single area of human life which is not holy, not inhabited by God.

"Theology is anthropology" was Feuerbach's famous motto. Meaning, partly, that you only have to study the sort of god a person worships, to get a good idea of how that person ticks. Listen to some of these religious leaders talking, and see what sort of image of God they conjure up. Then try to imagine what sort of parental/cultural tapes are running in their heads; in some strange way, they may not be talking about God at all, but rather, they are letting us have a glimpse of the magical figures from their past, who have moulded their present. "God" is just the glorification of their programming.

But Feuerbach's motto also suggests that it is by the study of the human concern that we will come to God-talk. To study humanity is to study its gods, but to discover about being human is to discover about God. As we learn to make our human journey in all the reality and complexity of the process that is us, so we will sense deep echoes of a connecting reality between ourselves and others, ourselves and creation. Somewhere there is a unity and a harmony. Somehow, however terrible it may be, we can trust what we experience. Each of us has his or her own story. That story is a gospel. When we learn to read it with truth, we will find that it shows us new meanings. And the gospel is Good News.

The donkey and the prophet ride off into the distance. They have a long way to go, and there will be many arguments on the journey. In time, perhaps they will learn to love each other. And when they have learned compassion for each other, perhaps when they have learned to enjoy the comedy of such an unlikely combination, then they will have work to do. Because there is a great city, where people suffer and live and die and go about their busy lives, caught in a treadmill of mere being. Outside the city waits Jesus – the man of blazing love and compassion; the voice of acceptance and forgiveness; the one who claims that all human life is touched with the divine. By his suffering and death, he will kindle a fierce light to say that never again can being be "mere" – life is too important, and the deepest questions of meaning and truth and value are involved in it. It is a battle to the death with the darkness; a battle with a surprising ending. But it cannot begin unless there is a donkey to carry him into the city.

There are donkey churches – a surprising number, in fact, but you don't hear very much about them, because being humble and vulnerable they don't make much of a song and dance about themselves. Their people have usually been put through the wringer at some time, and have learned to treat themselves and others with equal compassion. They have no doubt about the religious task. To be more, not less, human; to be more, not less, involved in the realities of life; to be more, not less, impatient with anything, including religion, that fails to take the human task seriously. They understand what it means to say that you have seen God at work in the powerlessness and failure of a man dying on a cross. If you look on a donkey's back, you will find that it is marked with a cross. Christian donkeys are marked by the cross too. It is no easy task to carry love.

Their silent witness questions us; and so does the silent man waiting to take up his cross again. Every day is Palm Sunday, and Good Friday, and Easter Day. Every town, city, village and home is Jerusalem. Where are the donkeys who will carry Christ? Is it too late for the prophet to open his eyes and see God? How does your story begin?

Epilogue

The cinema slowly empties, and we shuffle back into the cold streets. The alien space monster was destroyed, and the heroine, still looking remarkably beautiful, has headed off into the sunset. Films can make it look so easy. They have a beginning, a middle and an end, and everything fits neatly into those boundaries. For us – well, we can't be sure where we are most of the time. Life is a lot too messy to fit into neat categories; tragedy? comedy? prologue? epilogue? beginning of the second reel? What we have is the Now, the present moment, and how we choose to live that moment. We cannot live our lives waiting expectantly for a happy ending.

I hope that this book won't ride off into the sunset, leaving you to return to the cold streets alone. If I have made any of the answers sound too easy, then you will know how phoney they must be. But there *are* answers – life is too short and too precious to waste on captivity. It was Nietzsche who said, "Your bad love to yourselves makes solitude a prison to you". Half the time, we don't have any clear idea of who we are, what we really want, or what we really feel; instead, it's just a sort of grey blodge, with us in the middle.

"Bad love" – lack of love, lack of compassion, lack of attention. Is it too late in our lives to suggest a new sort of religious quest – a quest to find the reality of what it means to be me, to be you? To live each moment NOW, as it is, with honesty, integrity and courage, not bowing down to all the golden calves that surround us. To take back possession of our own lives, and claim the ground, however tragic, desperate or comic, as our own.

I'm talking about ideals, of course, which we can never fully reach. But if we are asked to choose between the frozen life of hanging on, and the risky life of walking freely, don't we know which is most important? Freedom, love, courage . . . when Socrates was describing the ideal life and the ideal society, his friend Glaucon said, "Socrates, I don't believe that there is such a city of God anywhere on earth". Socrates replied, "Whether such a city exists in heaven, or ever will exist on earth, the wise man will live after the manner of that city, having nothing to do with any other; and in so looking upon it, he will set his own house in order."

We cannot make the streets less grey. But perhaps we can start to wonder what Jesus meant when he said, "the Kingdom of God is within you". When we have begun to find ourselves, then we will have begun to find the Kingdom. And perhaps we will remember that in the beginning, according to the Bible, God created the world, and life, and light, out of chaos and darkness. If there had been no chaos to reshape, would God have been able to create anything? Perhaps the chaos and darkness that we feel inside us are the place of creation where God is at work. Perhaps the road we walk can be holy ground, not a prison cell. Perhaps we can even begin to love our gaolers, and to set both them and ourselves free.

"This is not the end. It is not even the beginning of the end. But it is, perhaps, the end of the beginning. . . ."